THE CHIMERA

and Other Dark Poems

By Michael Perret

Published in the United States by Curious Corvid Publishing, LLC, Ohio.

Cover Design and illustrations by: Rad Studio, LLC © 2023, Mitch Green

Printed in the United States of America

Curious Corvid Publishing, LLC
PO Box 204
Geneva, OH 44041

ISBN: 978-1-959860-09-9

curiouscorvidpublishing@gmail.com

TRIGGER WARNING: This book depicts acts of violence including sexual assault.

Contents

TRIGGER WARNING: This book depicts acts of violence including sexual assault.

The Chimera

Now who has she come to admire?
Byron, and his brooding vampire…

Alexander Pushkin,
Eugene Onegin III.12

Chimaera [ky-meer-uh]: Three-headed monster of Greek mythology, part lion, part goat, part serpent; symbol of nature in its diversity.

Chimera [shi-mur-uh]: Hope or dream that is illusory or impossible to achieve.

ONE

The vampire, Smarra, is in New Orleans. They have come under cover of the fears and expectations of death that come with annual outbreaks of yellow fever. They encounter the wealthy son of a slaveholder, Charles Labelle, and invite him back to their hotel for dinner. At the dinner, the vampire brings out a slave they have just purchased and named Charlus, who tells his story of being captured and brought to the new world.

I.

Needing, as it were, to survive by crime,
Kidnapping, murder, drinking human blood,
Perverting nature, tasting the sublime —
What can I say, it's safer in the flood
Of port cities; above all, when disease
Sows confusion, and death is expected;
No one is safe, everyone's suspected,
And, as unhindered as the fetid breeze,
A vampire's free to grimly make its rounds.
Thus I found myself in the busy sounds
Of the French Quarter at least once a year;
The tale that follows started there, when I,
Patiently waiting for people to die,
Entertained myself with what I found near

II.

At hand — *slavery*. Slavery was flourishing;
And though I find that enslaved blood dirties
The vintage, I find *slavers* nourishing,
Their blood…I thrived in the 1830s
In New Orleans. I was at the slave block,
And spied an attractive young man… — "Hello!"
He said, when I appeared at his side. — "Oh?"
I feigned surprise. — "These are fresh from the dock.
Raw, undomesticated, brutal, *cheap!*
No, the going price is always too steep
For finished slaves. You have to buy them crude —
Oh, *pardonnez*, my name is Charles Labelle.
My father says that I talk too much. Well,
There I go again. Please, don't think me rude."

III.

— "Not at all. My name is Smarra." We shook.
The smell of flesh, sweat, perfume and cologne
Was thick. I could almost eat the air. — "Look,
That one's more dead than alive — skin and bone.
Who'd buy that? We're not cooking negro soup,
Like cannibals," he waved, "from Guadeloupe!
Imagine!" he laughed. "Maybe voodoos do."
I raised my hand and put in my bid. "You?!"
— "No, I'm not a 'voodoo.' I need a boy."
— "What for?" he asked almost disarmingly.
— "Join me for dinner," I pressed, charmingly,
And I'll show you." He was silent, not coy —
I'd say, *afraid* and surprised by desire — I sensed his
knees shake and his loins perspire.

IV.

Charles Labelle was scared, not a virgin, just
Still young, and averse to women, unsure
Like so many, of their course, of their lust
When it doesn't conform: *Prey*, as it were,
To *predators* — to decadent creatures
Like me. He accepted, and after we
Concluded our business and went to see
Up close our human property's features,
I took him back to my hotel to dine.
I assured him the meal would be divine.
New Orleans was ripe with fruits to be plucked.
Good taste and a lot of money were all
It took to make the forbidden fruit fall.
"The nectar, my friend, that's here to be sucked!"

V.

The meal was served in several rich courses.
I watched as he stuffed it in like a goose.
I encouraged him to talk. My sources
Are never aware that I've tied the noose,
That while I listen I watch their veins bulge,
That each question hides an urge to indulge,
That as I sit there pretending to eat
Shifting my food on my plate in deceit,
Inside my mouth I feel my tongue quiver —
— "My family's plantation is called Belle-Grave.
Sugar. We have 200 slaves. We gave
Some old ones to a small farm upriver,
But I was fine with it because I knew
I'd be sent to buy more." — "And here you flew!

VI.

Lucky me." — "Lucky you…So, what of that
Slave boy?" There was something rash in his eyes;
The wine-soaked pseudo-aristocrat.
I smiled and nodded at a servant. Cries
Broke out in the hallway, then he appeared,
Dressed in fine clothes, bathed, shaking head to foot.
— "There's nothing to fear, dear boy," and I put
Out my hand. — "Move boy!" Labelle volunteered.
He was drunk now, his father's little man.
The son of a stupid, violent clan.
I'd watched them for centuries — well, *hunted*…
If you could call it that — *fished*, I should say.
I got up and guided the boy — "This way…" —
To the table. I sighed. Labelle grunted.

VII.

"*Charlus* is your name now," I said. "Now eat — "
I spread out for him my untouched dinner.
He hesitated. I made our eyes meet —
We vampires have a voice that is *inner* —
Desire is its measure, emotions, needs…
Utterly betrayed, completely undone,
He was starved for food, but also for one
Of this new world who could hear him. Beads
Appeared on his eyelashes. — *Eat, proceed,*
I told him, *I'll translate,* and freed
From his silence, the plates of food ignored,
His story, dammed by incomprehension,
Began to break through — flow through the tension,
Till through me into the new world it poured.

VIII.

—You seem kind to me, but no, I refuse
To eat. I will never eat again—not
Of my own will, nor will I live. Abuse
This living corpse if you must. It is rot
That causes it to perspire, to excrete—
Not life, not growth. So, if you want this meat
Inside me, you will have to hold me down—
His lips, downturned in a defiant frown,
Were still. He spoke through a wall of dried tears.
I thought when I came in, you would eat me.
At this ritual, what use could I be?
I don't know this strange land, and what one hears...
Charles burst out laughing. —"That's like what I said!"
Coldly I blinked and slowly turned my head.

IX.

— *They stuffed my mouth with rags when they took me,*
And strapped my arms down and my legs with belts.
My eyes were uncovered, so I could see
Others, their bodies with bruises and welts.
We'd been warned, "Whole tribes become slave traders —
A horizon of boats filled with raiders — "
Still, we were surprised, or we would have fought —
What does it matter? They came — we were caught...
The first night on the trail there was no food.
The second, they offered — I shook my head.
The third, I tried to refuse, but instead
Of leaving me to myself to be chewed
Up from the inside, they forced me to live —
They beat into me what they had to give —

X.

On the boat it was the same, only worse.
We were bound with chains, not belts, and the smell —
I felt dead before, but now in a hearse
Buried alive, stowed, submerged in the swell
Of vomit and shit, of piss, sweat and tears —
Exposed to the sick, to pus, fetid breath —
Bodies expiring, succumbing to death —
No, when I saw the sailors eat, my fears
Were confirmed, they were evil spirits, dark
Times were upon the world, and on this ark
I would be fattened up and then eaten —
But I couldn't eat, I was too sickened,
And so, as I thinned the floggings quickened —
Routinely force-fed, routinely beaten —

XI.

We have a saying, the women say:
Most animals you can always escape,
But one animal always gets its way,
That animal is man — They spoke of rape —
— "What is this?!" Charles Labelle, against the flood.
"He hasn't touched his plate — Neither have you!
I didn't take you for a Yankee, true,
But…" — "Another drink, Charles, it thins the blood."
— "All this talking! But I know why we're here —
Of boys, I've had my fair share, Smarra, dear —
And why did you name him 'Charlus,' that's dumb —
Is it because you really want me? Well,
I'm rich! My daddy is Vilcor Labelle,
So…" I bit into his neck like a plum.

XII.

Not what I'd intended—I'd had a plan—
It did not involve bite marks on his neck.
—"His inner thigh. Not even doctors can
Look there without shame. They blink when they
check,"
I explained to Charlus after the fact.
I had meant, though, for him to see it all—
To see my fangs drop, my eyes fill with gall—
To see me inhuman, to see me (wracked
With bloodthirst) thrill to the depredation—
It's your choice, he'd heard, *death by starvation*,
Or—I bit my own wrist for him to taste,
And gnashed my words, "Charlus, what do you think?
The chalice is full if you want to drink…
Good boy…" Such moments should not go to waste…

TWO

Posing as doctor and assistant, Smarra and Charlus transport Charles Labelle's unconscious body back to his plantation (Belle-Grave) with the intention of consuming the whole family under the guise of treating a local outbreak of yellow fever. Smarra describes how they were born in a medieval pagan village, where their hermaphroditic nature was accepted as normal, and how they were turned by a vampire living as a priest when the inquisition came to burn the village. When they arrive at Belle-Grave, Smarra glimpses Minerva, the head house slave, experiences love at first sight and begins referring to her as their "chimera."

XIII.

—"Imagine, Charlus, a city of death.
Sidewalks and streets for the dead or dying,
Where the living tiptoe, holding their breath
And, anyway, most of them are lying—
Or call it a carnival of horrors,
Two seasons to their grim reaper's delight,
Summer and fall, with their annual blight,
As we pose as tourists or explorers
Come to see the dance of death, drink our fill,
Burden the corpse carts with kill after kill,
Under the cover of the Saffron Scourge...
But first, *to the country*, I have a plan—
We're leaving, with this half-emptied out man,
This nervous necropolis on the verge—"

XIV.

I somehow made sure that Charles still had some
Life in him when we boarded the steamboat.
Charlus had taken to his blood like rum,
Which I liked, but still for our plan to float
We needed self-control and Charles alive.
I told the captain he was sick, that I
Was a doctor, and, so the boy could die
At home which his family, might we contrive
To provide a quiet, *quarantined* room?
There was a price, of course, and through the gloom
(I could see, in the captain's eyes, the fear
When I mentioned the boy's *yellow* pallor)
He named a high one; the captain's valor
Was shaken, but steady enough to steer.

XV.

He'd been startled by the season's quickness.
Some years you could get as far as July
Before the dreaded rumor of sickness
Began to be heard… It was all a lie,
Of course, the "black vomit" had not yet come —
The cesspools and swamps had not yet exhaled
Their warm, humid breaths — but the ship had sailed.
Now the whole region was bound to succumb,
Supporting our story that Charles was sick,
That I'd been called, *but progress had been quick,*
And his soul was already at death's door
When I found him unconscious in his room.
It's Yellow Fever, if I may presume —
So, I've brought him home, I can't do much more —

XVI.

He's going to die, but I heard him moan
"Belle-Grave…" and I thought, "Charles Labelle, let's go –
Better not to die with strangers, alone
In a sickening port!" It is, you know –
Sickening. The Fever's arrived early.
Monsieur Labelle might even be its first
Victim. Let's hope he is also its worst!
Way out here, on this plantation, surely
You all will be safe, and can mourn your son
In peace – At least that's how I'd hoped the fun
Would begin. In reality, my speech
Was not so formal. Such is life and art…
Sometimes they merge, sometimes they come apart.
In my poem, though, I give due weight to each.

XVII.

We approached the plantation house at night.
–"Charlus," I said, "the echoes of mourning –"
(The hanging moss looked sad in the moonlight.)
"Poetic foreshadowing, a warning
To the reader, *as they say*: Our story
Will not end well for someone…But we'll keep,
As we drive this cart, and the mosses weep,
That to ourselves…The details are gory,
Or will we…?" –"Smarra, I'm thirsty." –"Me too,
Charlus, and tonight, *this* Labelle's for you,
Or what's left of him. You'll nurse him with care
While I tap another, on the sly. See,
The fever's *catching*, according to me!
First we'll infect them, then we'll drink them…" –
"There!"

XVIII.

Yes, it was Belle-Grave looming before us.
Neoclassical in its claims to style.
—"Indeed, what a 'charming sarcophagus!'
We'll make it our own, at least for a while."
I'd sent word ahead when we disembarked
Of the sick young man, and when we arrived
Some apprehensive slaves came and contrived
To light our way. Their torches smoked and sparked
But I doubt they grieved for their master's heir.
By the way they tilted back and the care
They took in holding their breaths, I could tell
They were afraid of the young man's body —
Unconscious, nearly dead, in a shoddy
Cart — fearful of what his lungs might expel...

XIX.

Yes, Charlus, they are all afraid to die...
Unlike you. Even when you were alive
You preferred death to servitude. Now my
Gift to you is that in death you shall thrive,
Immortal, no longer subject to time.
We're still subject to thirst, that sublime
Desire. It is our unnatural state
To want blood, the way mortals procreate,
Erotically — otherwise, you are free.
No, time is nothing, it doesn't matter.
Neither does God, that gossip and chatter
About the afterlife...Now, you can see
How even those light–skinned people are slaves
To concepts and slogans like 'Jesus Saves'...

XX.

And the world is also unjust, Charlus.
Nature feeds and fells, prey is preyed upon.
Mortality is its unconscious noose.
One minute they're here, the next they are gone.
This life is always coming and going –
Harmless if it continues unknowing,
An injustice if it becomes a tool.
The true 'vampires' are the fools like this fool,
Who suck the life out of slaves and misuse
Their labor to construct things like Belle-Grave –
Or worse, they take the slave's essence and save
It on paper to stake against their dues –
But the worst are Christians, and men like them,
Who call nature evil and who condemn

XXI.

It. I really hate Christians, this is why:
(And poetic license, dear reader, if
I didn't really share these things with my
New friend, and humor my dive off this cliff –
Does the artform not require digressions?
Commentary? Poetic compressions?
I've read my Pushkin who in turn had read
His Byron…Now you can read me instead!)
I was born a monster according to
The men of the cloth, and all their followers,
The easy to dupe, the Word swallowers,
For I was made with not one sex but two
Between my legs, parts both female and male,
And behind, the vestiges of a tail.

XXII.

My pagan village accepted me fine.
My mother nursed me, my father obeyed
The dictates of nature, its course was mine.
No one cursed my difference or was afraid.
Then when I was twenty, the priests appeared.
The Inquisition was the thing we feared!
When they found me out, my village was burned –
They would have burned me too, but I was turned –
He was a priest, or in a priest's attire.
I heard the word, "Quick!" then the taste of blood –
Then it all went black, then again the flood
Of light – On a heap, a communal pyre,
I awoke, so thirsty, so filled with hate –
My revenge was immediate, and great –

XXIII.

I'll stop there. Maybe one day I'll depict
My first blood bath in music or in verse
Or I'll paint it, whichever to inflict
With the strongest effect, the intended curse,
Because I've become, in its aftermath,
The muses' best whore, and a polymath,
The undead envy of every old Faust
Who cries, *"One more one hundred years to oust*
These demons from my mind, this need to know!
That's all I need not to die incomplete!
That's all I need to make these two ends meet!"
But life is too short and you are too slow
To be chasing chimeras, mortal man!
Vampires alone have the speed and lifespan –

XXIV.

Unless that chimera is mortal too.
Then the vampire finds their days and nights bound
By the same time that scrapes and bores into
Their beloved's face…At Belle-Grave I found
Such a creature standing in the doorway —
Perfection because she could do no wrong —
A mortal, but also one of the throng
Of stars because my love put her there — Say
What you will if you must, but vampires love,
And not in the confusing push and shove
Of men and women giving into sin —
We drink blood out of a prurient need,
But when we sire it's not an impure deed,
It's a glimpse of the timelessness within —

XXV.

My brush with the chimera was fleeting.
Her shadow disappeared between glances —
In its place the Labelle's mournful greeting
Entreated us with hasty advances
To cross the threshold into a great hall
That echoed with each and every footfall.
A girl resting her hand on a railing
Looked down at us — We also heard wailing —
That's where she went, to inform the mother…
But before us we had the patriarch,
(His name was Vilcor Labelle) and the stark
Contrast of a doctor, then one other
Young man of color, tall, and his sighs
Were audible from behind his gray eyes —

XXVI.

—"Vilcor, his chances aren't good," (hands to brows)
"But Yellow Fever…" the doctor wondered…
I forgot to mention that between bows,
And while outside the sky cracked and thundered,
Charlus and I had put on masks. —"His breath
Though, doctor, it smells, does it not, like death?"
—"If I may, Monsieur…" —"*Doctor.*" —"Pardon, yes,
That may be, but if I might, the egress
Of foul humors is not likely to be…"
Charlus, behold, after Charles, our first kill —
"…Related, rather, it's the *blood* that's ill.
You see…" *blah-blah-blah-* "…matter of degree…"
So, instead, of one that no one would miss
(The mother), he's first, my new nemesis.

XXVII.

—"My dear colleague," I interrupted him,
"Suffice it to say, that a prayer was said
At the cathedral by Père Antoine; grim-
Faced, the Spaniard said a prayer for the dead.
For to his eyes, this boy has the Fever.
By chance, doctor, are you a believer?"
—"Of course-" he tried to say. —"Monsieur Vilcor,"
I addressed the patriarch, "at the door
We were not properly introduced. I
Am Doctor Smarra, and this is my son,
Charlus, and heir. I'm so blessed to have one —
I have rushed yours home so that he might die
In your arms. In spite of whatever chance
There is of contagion, I thought…" (A glance

XXVIII.

Down at the son, then back to the father.)
—"Of course," Vilcor said, "he's more than my name,
He's my boy, but why do the fate's bother
Hounding *me*? I can feel them taking aim,
And hear their running knot—They mean to hang,
If not me then my future, like Hera
Hounding Hercules—It's a new era,
Perhaps, that's on the horizon. Harangue
The marching armies of fate if you must,
But it won't stop them—Incipient dust,
That's all we are to their empty campaign—
No town is safe, no rural hideaway—
No future's safe, posterity's in play—
And my last wager is nobody's gain—"

XXIX.

(Indeed, I clapped.) —"But, Papa, you have me."
(But I clapped too soon!) —"Why are you downstairs?"
—"To mourn my brother." —"Like Antigone,"
I dared, stealing Creon's thunder. —"Yes…Where's
Minerva?" I was about to laugh when
She appeared, my chimera, there again—
She was fifty, exquisite, high cheekbones—
Bright brown, deep amber, rich and tight skin tones
Drawing her eyes into exotic slits,
And lips where I thought I caught her bemused,
By herself and others being abused
By buffoons, but also used to their fits.
I said, *Hello*, but she didn't respond—
"Minny, take Lucy up!" Lucy was blond.

XXX.

"Forgive my daughter, she's sixteen, a child
Still, in need of a husband, truth be known..."
—"Not at all," I could see that he was riled.
—"Doctor Smarra, I must leave you alone
For the moment. Apollo, take Charles and
The doctor to the large guest room, as planned.
Then find a room for Smarra." —"And the slave?"
—"I'm sure there's room in their little enclave
Out back somewhere. Get Brontes to take him."
—"If I may, Monsieur—!" I started to say,
But Charlus stopped me. *Smarra, it's okay.*
I want to see the slave quarters — The dim
Glimmer of the entrance hall candles glowed,
Cloaking the fires that in our eyes showed—

THREE

Smarra slips out into the night from his lodging to find the family physician (the next victim). They find them nursing Charles Labelle, and are still biting the doctor when Venus, the slave-mistress of Vilcor Labelle, shows up, needing to speak with Charles. She reveals her plot to kill Vilcor with Charles's and Apollo's help. Apollo and Charles would then run away to Paris with the latter's inheritance, while Venus, having had her son by Vilcor legitimized, would stay and inherit Belle-Grave. Smarra sings a love song (sensing that Minerva is spying outside the door) and then bites Venus.

XXXI.

Apollo, the young man of color, found
A room for me in another building.
The *garçonnière* it's called, for *garçons* bound
By custom to the decadent gilding
Of male privilege. In those days, in those dens,
That meant gambling and discussing money,
Bad jokes about girls, none of them funny,
Too much drinking, and too much time with friends
Sometimes, when over the fourth glass of port,
Through the cigar smoke, a harmless retort
Was mistaken for a slight of honor —
Then the two friends would dance and each dancer
Would fire their gun demanding an answer.
(Reader, in duals, *mankind's* the real goner —)

XXXII.

But as you know, I am no *garçon*, so
I wasted no time in slipping back out.
A slave tried to hide his pipe's furtive glow.
Shh, I gestured. —"Ain't seen no one about,"
He sighed assuringly. A cloud of smoke
Hung in the wet and heavy air, each toke
Only added to the undispersed haze
Of rich undifferentiated grays.
I've tasted the blood of slaves, like I said,
But have a *penchant* for the slaveholder's.
As this slave in my memory smolders,
I think I should have just killed him instead
Of leaving him there, a bit of his eye
Still on me…No doubt, acting as *her* spy—

XXXIII.

But I'm getting ahead of myself, first
The doctor succumbed to the infection.
I was there, I felt the artery burst
In his upper inner thigh. *Perfection!*
If I may: I snuck up behind my prey
As he was bent over his patient (Charles).
I sensed him start at my unrepressed snarls,
And his legs just barely begin to splay,
When I lunged and lanced his saphenous vein,
Sucking so hard it barely left a stain,
Until he was quite unconscious and still.
Then I heard my name—"Smaaaaraaa"—and, still dazed
From slaking my hellish thirst, (*God be praised!*
Charles is awake!) I drank another fill.

XXXIV.

I mean, Labelle woke up, against all odds.
Sorry, Charlus, I thought. *I had no choice.*
As I arranged the bodies (my façades
Are always convincing), I heard a voice
In a whisper I hadn't heard before:
−"Let me go!" −"Shhh!" −"I have to speak to him!"
I put on my mask, and straightened a limb,
Then glided over and opened the door.
Minerva, proud, indignant, coldly met
My welcoming eyes. I'll never forget
How she took my "Bonsoir" with one quick nod,
(I'd caught her spying; the fault wasn't hers,
She'd been given away by amateurs),
And left me to, some say, a lesser god...

XXXV.

Venus. That was her name. Perhaps it's time
To insist that these ridiculous names
Are not my invention−They're hard to rhyme!
No, Vilcor himself was behind these games.
He treated his slaves like toy figurines,
And if he liked you, and you had the means,
As Venus did, in her body, he might
Make you his favorite, at least for the night.
He might even recite some Ovid first!
I learned such things, and more from Venus. −"Please,
Doctor, is Charles awake?" −"I don't think he's..."
I took her hand to avoid an outburst
In the hallway. "If I may be so bold,
Mademoiselle..." −"Oh! But your hand is so cold!"

XXXVI.

—"Not so loud! They've all been upset enough—
Come in, but beware, and cover your face.
The chill in this tomb, I mean, room, could snuff
Out the very flame that keeps hope apace
And able to catch us in our despair.
You'll find him across the room—over there—
But he has long since ceased to breathe, my dear.
And on the divan, unconscious, I fear,
Your family physician has met his fate.
Even if in his chest I still detect
Some life, my training leads me to suspect
That's it's only a flicker. It's too late.
Surprised by a plague too few understand
He's been ordered back into death's remand—"

XXXVII.

—"What?" —"Charles is dead. The doctor's good as
dead.
And now you too shall join th-" —"Oh, no! He can't!
You can't die!" —"But-" She ran to his deathbed
And drummed on his chest with her fists. The pant
From *her* chest, mind you, awakened my thirst
Again, but, dear reader, there's more to me
Than a thirsty old vampire debauchee.
Nothing gets me more than a plot well versed.
Nothing wards off the ennui and fatigue
Of eternal life like some good intrigue,
And I'd caught its scent, so I stoked its fire.
"Indeed, love can be a difficult game...
And I'd thought Apollo, though of the same..."
—"Charles and me?! *No*. Him? *Yes*. Him and this *liar*!

XXXVIII.

They had plans to run away to Paris,
Paradise on earth, apparently, while
I would stay and become Labelle's heiress,
Having been freed, before Vilcor's..." A smile
Bent her lips. —"Accident...?" —"Well...okay, *yes!*
Charles would convince him to free me and bless
The fruit of our union with his proud name.
Then he'd fall off his horse —or something lame —
Charles and Apollo would then take their share
And leave the rest to my Cupid and I —"
—"Cupid...?" —"Vilcor's son." —"I see and that's
why..."
—"Oh, doctor, this is more than I can bear!
His illegitimacy, my disgrace —
They say I'm colored, but look at this face!"

XXXIX.

Indeed, she had not heeded my advice,
And covered her face; and I must admit
I'd assumed she was white, though the precise
Schematic of races is counterfeit
Science, even today, but *"when in Rome"*.
—"Tragic," I said. —"I should *not* be a slave!
I am appropriately named though, save
I prefer the Greek to the Roman: *Foam,
Aphros, Aphrodite*, but I'm Venus."
—"Deserved, regardless of race or genus,"
I agreed, removing my mask. "But, dear,
Remember that these walls have ears. I saw —"
—"You mean Minerva? Ha! That old jackdaw!"
—"Well, then," I said, "you have nothing to fear..."

XL.

But I thought I could feel my blackbird's eye
Peering through the keyhole and sense her ears
Tuned to us. Venus spoke, but so did I.
She told me, indignantly, how for years
She'd learned the same lessons as her master.
"Lucy?" — "Yes, only I learned them faster!
We were raised like sisters, but she's so bland,
I mean, insipid, that her father's hand
Prefers to pet me — But if you must judge
Somebody, *she's* the one who let those boys
Experiment with her privates like toys —
I guess they needed to be sure..." — "The grudge
She must hold against them." — "Whatever. Slut."
— "I have a grudge, I'd like to share, but...

XLI.

Well, you shouldn't have referred to my love
As a 'jackdaw,' because I must confess,
I can't fathom, from below or above,
A more perfect creature. A poetess
Once sagely composed a song for her *beau*
Or *belle*, the gender's unclear, where she sings:
To be beloved is to be all things
To be perfect when imperfectly so
Because imperfection is part of you
And my love's all-encompassing and true.
Let them say you're too dark — your darkness glows —
Let them go deeper into your abyss —
I come with a supernatural bliss
Where limitless fulfillment overflows..."

XLII.

I'd addressed that song to Minerva, not
To Venus. No, vampires do not have sex —
We sire by turning — True sometimes it's hot,
Sometimes so inflamed that it even wrecks
Our judgment, sometimes the fallout is dire —
The walk (in my case, crawl) of shame applies
To us too, but, Hark, my pen, how it flies
And gets ahead of my tale — Now, admire
Venus, believing she had me seduced,
Unaware of what she'd really produced,
Merely by breathing and making me wait
While she vented. — "Monsieur, I *can't*...Vilcor..."
— "Is a dead man, don't worry, you'll get your...
Just desserts..." I knelt. "Now, make this leg straight..."

XLIII.

I straightened out the veins in her thigh and drank
A nectar of the gods beyond compare.
I filled my mouth, swallowed, then licked and sank
My teeth back in — *the door?* — I didn't care.
I could kill them all in one night, but stop
I couldn't — not until my thirst was quenched —
But once I mastered myself and had wrenched
My tongue away from the holes and the sop
Of her garter, I checked. The door *was* locked.
I surveyed the room and tried to concoct
A scenario for three bodies drained.
I did my artful best and hung a sign
As I slinked away drunk and serpentine:
FETID EXHALATIONS! MUST BE CONTAINED!

FOUR

*Leaving Venus and the doctor half dead, Smarra goes looking
for Charlus in the slave quarters out back. Charlus comes
running out from the woods afraid and informs Smarra that
the slaves at Belle-Grave practice voodoo. He describes the
beginning of a ritual sacrifice he witnessed and believes they
have the power to kill vampires and intend to kill them. He
also describes his failed attempt to turn a condemned slave.
Charlus also explains to Smarra the logic of living sacrifice.
That the more potential for evil a creature has, the more potent
the sacrifice. A venomous snake possesses some potential
ability to cause harm, but a human being, and most potently, a
white male baby has the most potential ability to cause harm,
as proven by the slave trade.*

XLIV.

Behind their pillars and their pilasters
Behind their poor pantomimes of the Greek
Behind the mock temple of the masters,
I found, lit only by the smoking reek
Of cheap torches, a prison *en plein air*.
I saw men chained to posts, trying to sleep --
I could smell the dried blood, the silent weep --
I felt the apathy and the despair.
Charlus, I thought to myself, then I cried,
-- *Charlus!*, but he didn't answer. Inside
Two rows of small brick houses I could hear
Suspicion mounting amongst the awake,
But down the alley I moved like a snake,
Blithe by nature. I had sensed him near.

XLV.

—*Smarra!* — *Charlus!* Alright, I admit it,
I'd begun to worry—he was so young—
And, in fact, it feels right to commit it,
My parental instinct, to these lines, sung
Out of a desire to make myself known.
Does it not come from our being alone
That we turn our private thoughts into art?
And who is more alone, more set apart
Than me? Monstrous, when I was still human;
At least for a short time there at the end,
When the priests came. Since then, I've had to fend
For myself, and flutter, like a numen,
In the spaces in-between your fixed views,
Where I meet with and fuse with your taboos—

XLVI.

— *Smarra, it's not safe here. We have to go.*
I followed Charlus into some dark woods.
—*What is it, Charlus?* I asked. The moon's glow
Was cloaked by the mist, the moss, the close hoods
Of old trees, but still, I showed him the way
By other means, some natural, some
Beyond that and exceeding the spectrum
Of the possible. — *Smarra, listen, they
Know. They knew enough to distrust my tale,
And enough, in advance, to countervail
My attempt to make one of them like us…*
I knew it. — *Charlus, you are still too young!*
— *Yes, Smarra, I know that now, but they've hung
Sacrifices, in their huts — from the truss,*

XLVII.

Chickens and snakes bleeding out into bowls –
I remember such things worshiped back home.
They are dark, Smarra, with powerful goals!
They're possessed and cake their bodies with loam!
They dance! – Charlus, I interrupted him,
Again you forget what we are to them.
We are the monsters, the things to be feared.
Their superstition, whatever they've smeared
On their bodies, or the walls, won't protect
Their bodies or their souls. They pray – we reign
Like gods! Charlus! Why forget your disdain
For life now, when, as one of the elect,
You cannot die? Trust me! – No, Smarra, you
Trust me, and don't disregard this voodoo!

XLVIII.

When I left you there in the entrance hall,
That giant, Brontes, took me around back.
He was quiet, he spoke hardly at all –
I noticed that most of his teeth were black.
Before he took me to the other slaves,
Who I meant to raise from their living graves,
I admit it, and free them, like you did
For me, we stopped to wait, when someone slid
Out from the shadows and asked me my name.
It was that house slave. – Minerva? – Yes, her.
I repeated our story, but the blur
Clouding her eyes made it clear that our game
Had not convinced her – then she took my hand
*And read my palm…*Which is what she had planned

XLIX.

All along! I've learned, *Bohemians* know —
I don't know how, but the gypsies can read
In these lines how they do *not* come and go —
That we are *not* exactly alive — freed
Somehow from the usual fate...They're brave.
I lived with some in the old country, moved
With them constantly; they always proved
True to our deal: I protected and gave
Freely of all my victims' possessions —
They kept me and my bloody transgressions
Like a cult. *Some of them must have passed through...*
And taught these people about the vampire...
Suddenly I felt a rush of desire —
She knows what I am! I felt so close to

L.

Her at that moment of recognition!
— *Charlus, continue. What else did she say?*
— *Nothing, just a look...but the omission*
Said it all. Then she turned and went away.
While I imagined my chimera's bright
Blue tignon, her forehead, deep bronze and smooth,
And her knowing eyes and how they could soothe
Me in seeing me, Charlus's long night,
Muffled in the background, progressed in words
That reached my ears mixed with the songs of birds
In the distance and all the insects' din —
None of it was able to pierce my dream,
Gently drifting on the swamp fog and steam
That filled the dark woods we found ourselves in —

LI.

Then Brontes led me to that avenue –
You saw it – two rows of buildings, a dirt
Road between them and a square where a few
Men bound in chains, left exposed and inert,
Languished – prey to heat, insects and the rain.
I'll revive them, I thought, I would return –
The passion in my eyes began to burn –
I'd free them, relieve them of all this pain –
I shut my eyelids, averted my gaze.
I distrusted Brontes now, and the blaze
Catching fire within was rattling my core.
I was trembling when we reached my dwelling
For the night, when, with a wave compelling
Me through, I entered, and he closed the door.

LII.

"I will get you some food," I heard him say,
But I also heard him lock me inside.
I wasn't afraid, I knew that my stay,
Or at least its length, was mine to decide.
Forced to run through the brush, tied up in knots,
Chained down in the hull in contorted lots
Like uniform wares, in a robber's bed –
(Procrustes's) – no, that windowless shed
Didn't frighten me, though I felt the stitch
In my side of having been led there and caged…
I gave the storm that inside me still raged
A moment to pass, as I, through the pitch-
Black discerned with supernatural eyes
An alter strewn with bones of every size –

LIII.

I forced the door open, breaking the lock
Like sealing wax snapped on a secret note.
I'd fled that alter, but now the whole block
Seemed to whisper save for a bleating goat —
Then drums joined the murmur — I saw a light —
A flicker from behind a curtain — They
Were sacrificing things, Smarra — They —
Listen to me! I saw one of them bite
Into a live snake and drain all its blood
Over his face, down his chest in a flood
That aroused me…until a baby's cry
Set off shouts of the words: "Cabrit sans cor!"
— Ah, I translated, "Chèvre sans cornes", or
"Goat without horns." — Precisely, Smarra! I

LIV.

Recalled the ways of the witches and priests
Back home, how their offerings were tiered,
From the highest to the lowest beasts,
On the potential evil that inhered
In each one's future, destiny or fate.
A viper can cause only so much harm,
But a man…and as we learned with alarm,
A white man, the evil he could create
Surpassed what we thought possible…The real
Danger, at first, was that we could not feel
The reality of the things we saw
In our bones — it was all beyond belief —
But out of our confusion, fear and grief
We glimpsed a power from which we could draw…

LV.

But there weren't many white babies out there,
And the mixed children from rape had no hope.
The 'goat without horns' became a mere prayer,
A legend, a threat we muttered to cope
With the crimes that swept us up in their storm.
A pure white baby, its evil untapped,
Bought stealthily, or brutally kidnapped
To be offered up against the great swarm
Of light-skinned demons... – Charlus, witches lie
Almost as much as priests, they mystify...
– They have their reasons! – There's nothing to fear!
Though I will say this, I've drunk the pure blood,
I've squeezed the juice out from the raw rosebud,
And I prefer it aged, sinful, severe...

LVI.

– No, Smarra. A woman entered, breasts bared.
She held up the baby, danced around, spat –
The drummers beat faster, but they looked scared
When she stopped them, "It's time – Bring me the bat!"
Somehow I knew that they meant to kill me.
– "Mean to" and "can," Charlus! Two different things!
– I ran, but first I snapped the chains, like strings,
That bound one of those men in the street. "Flee
With me!" I whispered, and dragged him along.
"Listen to me, brother, you don't belong
Here. You're guilty of nothing. Never doubt
The world's rotten, through and through, it's corrupt –
Running's not enough, you have to disrupt
It's hold on your nature, inside and out –

LVII.

I can free you." He looked at me, confused.
Then I bit my wrist, my eyes burning red –
"Drink this," I said. "Drink it!" But he refused –
We were in the woods, it was dark, I pled –
I tried to force his lips closer to me –
But he found his voice and screamed, "Chòvsourit!"[1]
I covered his mouth with my bleeding wrist.
He struggled, his muffled voice groaned and hissed.
Then overwhelmed...Smarra, I must have dreamed
I was kissing his neck, for when I woke
My mouth was full, and I wanted to choke –
I coughed up his blood – it splattered – I screamed,
"No! It's better this way!" and I shook him.
"Trust me!" but he was limp in every limb –

LVIII.

I dragged his body to the swamp, then heard
You calling, so I ran back to warn you –
To save you, because you saved me. You blurred
The boundaries, showed me another way through –
Not life, not death, immortal...unliving.
And when the world is as unforgiving,
As hostile and harsh to what I'd call life
As it is today, with strife upon strife,
I long to invite the ones bound in chains,
Tied up with rope and defined by bad laws
To explore the dormant fangs in their maws
And free themselves from the slaveholder's reins –
But, Smarra, tonight we have to escape
Before their new plan has time to take shape!

---

[1] "Bat!" (Haitian Creole)

LIX.

— We're here to feed, Charlus, not to save the world!
*And we cannot die…*at least not that way…
But I didn't say it. My fingers curled
Around his as we held hands, as the day
Began to break and we reached my lodging.
I know what you're thinking, perhaps the sun
Would burn us to ashes, but no, that one
Isn't real. Vampires don't dash off dodging
The rays of the sun like flaming arrows —
Crouching in corners, squeezed into narrows —
If you must know, we are like lizards, cold —
But unlike them, we are empty and dry.
Parched and shaking in the sun's warmth, could I
Combust…? Well, from such scenes, folklores get told.

FIVE

The next morning, Apollo brings Smarra an invitation from the Labelle family to have breakfast with them. When Smarra goes they are surprised to find the family (Vilcor, his wife, and daughter Lucy) already dressed in mourning. They inform them that Charles died in the night and the physician and Venus have run away. Smarra is confused. Vilcor offers to take Smarra for a tour of the plantation.

LX.

The potential lifespan of a vampire
Is endless, or, as long as there's vital
Ichor to fill empty veins, the desire
To *drink*, or, under its other title,
Live, will be there. Melancholy's rare —
And we are exceedingly hard to kill...
Sometimes like a human, I wonder still
About the beyond, the black *somewhere* where
We go when *we* die...*But we are like gods!*
I laugh, and my imagination nods
At scenarios like the end of life
On this planet with all its dried-up husks,
Immobile, blind to the mornings and dusks
Casting gray tides on the undeads' unlife —

LXI.

Lugubrious, I know, but, such is love,
Which among vampires is like for a child.
We love, we turn, we sire and we're proud of
Our pups, born into darkness, and reviled.
It was morning, when suddenly the door
Rattled, and Charlus, just as quickly, hid.
I should mention the tray, the untouched lid,
Someone had left for me the night before.
I'd neglected to dissemble that meal,
And now an interest he could not conceal
Caused Apollo to stare at it, working,
From the doorway with a new tray in hand,
Through possible explanations. He scanned
My quarters, but — "There's only *me* lurking..."

LXII.

I invited him in to leave the tray,
Bearing coffee, some flowers and a note.
"From Vilcor," I said. "Apollo, please stay —
'*Come for breakfast — Pardonnez —* ' quote/unquote.
You can tell Vilcor, '*T'would be my pleasure!*'
And that there's something important we need
To discuss. Ah, you look nervous, indeed...
But as a being accustomed to leisure,
(Not excluding venereal delights,
The lusts that *Venus* inspires and excites —
All of them), and as a doctor, of course,
Privacy is something that I respect.
Perhaps I knew Charles in ways you suspect...?
Oh well, I'm not one to pry or to force...
I abhor the indiscrete and the coarse."

LXIII.

"Charlus," I said, when Apollo was gone,
"Don't worry, he's just jealous and afraid
I'll reveal their plot to Vilcor. I'm on
To him. He is right though, Venus, betrayed
It all to me...the fool, dancing with death,
Inviting it — *me* — inside. Her last breath
Awaits you. Finish her off, the man too.
I didn't intend it, but there are two.
I'm going to breakfast — Just don't get caught!
And listen-" — "Smarra-" — "No, I must have her!
Each second she's not immortal's a blur —
Things *are* moving more quickly than I thought,
But we can't leave yet. I must turn her first!"
He shook his head. "Now, go! and slake your thirst!"

LXIV.

Where was she? My chimera — the most feared,
At least by Charlus...and yet, it was true.
I meant to address her when she appeared,
Minerva, my mambo, queen of voodoo.
At the table sat Vilcor and his wife,
Their daughter ('Antigone'), all in black.
The doctor's presence...we all felt the lack
Of that as yet undisclosed loss of life,
But I had a story, ready and pat:
He must have made his rounds exactly at
The wrong time, for at the moment of death
They have found that when the patient expires,
Tragically, from every orifice, spires
Of toxins emanate with the last breath...

LXV.

*And...*but they were already in mourning...
– "I'm so sorry," I said, "you're all in black..."
– "Hastily. We only learned this morning...
We might need you." – "Of course," taken aback,
Or feigning to be. "Charles?" – "Yes, in the night.
And the doctor..." – "Him too?!" – "No, he took flight!"
– "Lucy!" her mother said. – "And Venus, too!"
– "Venus, too...?" – "You see, we might just need you,
As a physician," Vilcor continued.
"Though with Charles dead and no one else sick..." –
"Yet."
He shrugged. "I understand. Of course." – "You'll get
His room." – "Near mine. They'd hoped we'd marry."
– "Rude,
Lucy!" her mother hissed. – *Not that old leech!*"
I laughed, though, in truth, who was I to preach!

LXVI.

– "I thought, to minimize our time indoors,
Perhaps, you'd enjoy a tour. Do you ride?"
– "Why, yes." – "My husband gives wonderful tours."
– "I'm sure he does." – "He's a wonderful guide."
I smiled at Lucy. – "All of us, I hope."
– "No, they'll be fine. Women know how to cope
With disease. They're closer – would you agree? –
To mortality, to nature, while we
Men, like the heroes of old, storm the skies.
And though like Bellerophon, yes, man falls,
And sometimes in the desert, yes, man crawls
On all fours – *Look there!* – and see how man tries
Again for the heavens! Yes, such is man:
High-minded and striving as best he can."

LXVII.

— "Such beautiful words, dear." — "Indeed, encore!
(I recommend lunch on the *galerie*),"
(To the ladies), but then back to Vilcor,
"Yes, 'such is man,' I wouldn't disagree:
A failure, a recurring lifetime's worth
Of falling, head over ass, back to earth —
Pardon. Whereas women have something rare
And supernatural tucked inside there —
Love, unconditional, for the *unseen*,
Regardless of what abnormality
Might come offending what morality...
Perhaps, Madame, understands what I mean —
Love has the power to find perfection
Where others find just cause for rejection."

LXVIII.

— "Yes, I never liked the songs Charles would sing
With Apollo, all painted up like blacks.
What a performer...Oh dear, what a thing..."
— "They wanted to move to Paris, their packs
Filled with sheet music, perfume...my dresses..."
— "Lucy, leave the table!" — "Oh, but mother,
You bore me inside there, like my brother!
Aren't I perfect, as Monsieur professes?"
I bristled at that *'Monsieur.'* — *I'm no male!*
I flung at her and risked letting the veil
Fall from her eyes and my disguised face. *See,*
Antigone, I'm more monster than man!
We'll talk later. Then aloud, I began,
"As for Bellerophon, it seems to me...

LXIX.

That his story is more about the fear
That men have of women, of birth and death,
Of mortality. He would rather steer
Pegasus upwards than face the hot breath —
Breaths, I should say, not one, for *she* had three,
Of the Chimaera, multiplicity
Incarnate, nature, impure and diverse,
Who to his eyes appeared obscene, perverse
And finally, inescapable, so
The hero stormed heaven, wanting to hide,
From that great truth, up Jupiter's backside —
But the monster he'd yoked and forced to go,
Inspired by the Chimaera, bucked its charge,
And forsook him to wander on the marge..."

LXX.

Before I continue, I should confess
To a modification of this myth,
Which I have pondered, at times, to excess,
And used to illustrate my morals with.[2]
In my version Pegasus falls in love
With the Chimaera, and in her six eyes
Sees his wings reflected, their fall and rise,
And accepts that he's a monster too. Of
Such *reverses* it has sometimes been said,
Let the ancients have their myths and instead
Of rewriting theirs come up with your own!
But I believe in correction and change,
And I don't find it in the least bit strange
To show through their myths what else can be shown.

---

[2] See *Appendix: Pegasus in Love*

42

LXXI.

So, on I went about how the winged horse,
Pierced by Cupid's arrow (rather than stung
By Jupiter's gadfly) reared up, changed course,
And, having found his monstrosity, flung
Bellerophon down. "Love is a mirror —
A mother in her child's eyes — queerer
Still, a lover in their beloved's..." *You*
Minerva, I thought...When Vilcor broke through,
"Monsieur-" — "M." — "Pardon?" — "Just *M. Smarra*, not
Monsieur." — "Just M...How literary. Well,
Doctor, shall we? From your plate I can tell
That you're not hungry." — "No, I have a knot
In my stomach, it seems. Yes, some fresh air,
I think." I muttered, pushing back my chair.

SIX

Riding horses with Vilcor, they see a slave digging Charles's grave at the family graveyard. Vilcor informs Smarra that that very morning Minerva implored him to legitimize Cupid (his baby with Venus). Smarra wonders if this is an attempt to make Cupid's sacrifice more potent. Smarra lies to Vilcor, claiming that they were a friend of Charles's in New Orleans and had tried to keep him out of trouble, but he was debauched. They then offer to marry Lucy. They are both surprised by a zombie slowly moving towards them. From its wounds, Smarra recognizes it as the condemned slave Charlus had told him about.

LXXII.

As Vilcor and I rode out, my thoughts went
Back to Charlus, the two bodies, regret
That I'd missed Minerva and instead spent
The morning pretending to eat *omelette*.
— "These horses remind me of your reading.
Pegasus *is* a monster," Vilcor said,
"And hovers, heavy-bodied, overhead
Like a false god...*Art* perhaps...? Conceding
Your point..." My mind strayed to the Spanish moss
That hung, gray and still, like a shroud across
The oak grove, when a familiar slave
Came into view. — "Is that Brontes?" — "Ah, yes.
Miss Minny, Belle-Grave's true proprietress,
Already has him digging my son's grave..."

LXXIII.

—"Minerva, you mean?" I tried to discern
In the hole in progress room for two more.
—"Miss Minerva, yes, my wife's taciturn
Slave companion from childhood. Let's explore
The sugar fields—This way—She does it all,
Especially with the slaves. When they brawl,
She has them whipped. When—*if*—they try to run
Or pilfer, well, she has eyes like the sun—
She sees all. Why, this morning—" then, he paused.
We'll come back to that, I thought, then I sighed
Loudly. —"I have a confession…I lied
Last night…I did know Charles—knew him well—
caused
Him, on occasion, to extend his stay
In the dangerous, depraved, *Vieux Carré*…

LXXIV.

I was his friend, but you must believe me,
I loved him and wanted to keep him safe.
Social positions, perhaps you'll agree,
Have their…vintages, and Charles…every waif,
Free or enslaved…well, he wanted a taste—
Even as we implored him, '*Charles, don't waste
Your privileges and gifts on all these boys
From other races!*'—but he loved his toys…"
—"Oh, don't judge him so—like father like son—
What if I told you that I am the same.
Would you try to save me as well? or blame
Me for what I've done—what I've left undone
As a father…as Miss Minerva did,
This morning, with *him* in her arms." —"Cupid?"

46

LXXV.

He nodded. — *"'You still have a son, accept*
His legitimacy and your duty
As the patriarch!' Then, surprised and swept
Up in her indignance and dark beauty
I swore I'd draw up the papers today —
I'd free Cupid, recognize him as heir
To whatever the slave laws shall declare
Legal, once his status has changed." — "Delay
That," I inserted, detecting a ruse
To increase the baby's potential dues
To the devil in privilege and power...
Not that I believed in those "goats without horns,"
Or sin, or a witch's claims to newborns,
Sacrifices at the witching hour...

LXXVI.

But where was Charlus? and the other two?
I was treading cautiously, "My advice —
I mean, forgive me if I treat you,
Out of habit, like Charles — *that* sacrifice
Would corrupt your blood and sever your line.
You still have Lucy, and though her presumed
Groom has vanished, she need not be entombed
With her brother." — "Oh, Lucy, I'd confine
Her to a convent but...those poor nuns..." — "Yes,
Charles would speak of her sometimes. I confess,
Perhaps my love for him influenced me,
But before even meeting her I felt
Something...and sometimes, as my thoughts would melt
Into dreams, I'd imagine her, what she...

LXXVII.

Was like in real life." Out of the corner
Of his eye, Vilcor now watched me, intrigued.
No longer the inadequate mourner,
He dropped the mask, exposing the fatigued
Patriarch whose progeny had vexed him,
Tragically turning his oversexed limb
Into a source of frustration and fear —
A mortal reminder that death was near,
A weariness hounding his every day.
"I could not save Charles, but I can save her,
And perhaps in so doing, see you blur
Into focus somewhere safe, far away
From this epidemic about to burst —
It *will* take its toll before its dispersed — "

LXXVIII.

Vilcor raised one hand, then for gravity,
Closed his eyes in an effort to contain
His gleeful, self-centered depravity.
I lowered my eyes to hide my disdain.
— "You wish to marry my daughter, correct?
And recommend I travel to avoid
Catching this fever? I admit I've toyed
With the idea…You say you suspect…"
— "I suspect this year's plague will be severe.
And believe me when I say, I revere
The Labelle name and want only to save
The memory of Charles, and Lucy's soul,
And, perhaps, you too — or, at least, console
A father before his son's open grave — "

LXXIX.

Vilcor coughed and nodded, and, reaching, squeezed
My arm warmly. — "Monsieur—or—M.—Young man,
You look so young and yet—" but then he seized
His reins in fear, and, with his horse, began
To slowly back away. A moment's pride
Filled my empty chest. Suddenly it burned,
Like living lungs deprived of air it yearned
To be flooded with blood, tide upon tide—
Had my true self unwittingly appeared?
My fangs dropped? No, I was not what he feared:
Almost in a whisper, he said one word,
And pointed, eyes wide, over my shoulder:
"Voodoo!" I looked and my chest grew colder.
Over the still hush, its moans could be heard—

LXXX.

A zombie...I'd never seen one before—
Covered in powder or ash, head to foot.
Its mouth was open, at its neck the gore
Caused by Charlus had been stitched up and put
In order...*It's the slave he'd tried to free!*
— "Yes, it's a local remedy," I said,
"For the Fever. Charlus, my...slave, who bled
One last night for rheum, explained it to me—
It's preventative." — "Thank God, there's a priest
On his way." — "A what?!" Of course, the deceased
Attracted priests like flies. I thinned my lips.
"Perfect. I'll share my feelings with Lucy
Soon." He was starting to look too juicy...
I daydream drank him in warm little sips—

LXXXI.

But satisfied myself with some cruel news
Of my own in non sequitur. "Of course,
It's better that she's gone. Who? *Venus*. Coups
Are best handled through exile." — "Coup?" His horse
Stopped. — "Oh, Monsieur Labelle, you didn't know?
I was sure it was you who made her go!
It was Apollo, who I was surprised
To find at my doorstep, skeletonized
With dread. You weren't aware of their plot?" —
"Dread?
Plot?" — "To have you killed — to flee to Paris —
To become the Labelle's heir and heiress
Through crime and the help of your son...I pled
With him to think it through. 'Don't be a fool!'
But he hated 'papa'...and loved that ghoul."

LXXXII.

— "Apollo?" — "Who else? But now it makes sense,
Why he's still up at the big house serving
Breakfast. But Venus, what of her absence?
Well, with Charles dead, she'd think of preserving
Herself first by seducing Lucy's groom!
She must have had a few tricks, she seduced — "
— "Yes, yes." — "And subsequently, she produced — "
— "Cupid, yes. We should speak to Minny." — "Whom
You will ask to take care of Apollo...?"
I was of two minds, whether to follow,
And approach my chimera, or to find
Charlus — I was beginning to worry —
Zombies, priests, voodoo "goats" in a hurry
Had been unleashed. I politely declined.

SEVEN

Smarra finds Lucy in the drawing room. They are surprised to find her mother there too, but then notices that Madame Labelle is wearing a gris-gris around her neck that protects her mind from Smarra's telepathic abilities. Smarra then has a telepathic conversation with Lucy, while throwing inane pleasantries at her mother. Lucy describes her rape by her brother and Apollo, and how she became pregnant, though the baby was still born. She also indicates how this experience has freed her from conventional morality. Smarra is overjoyed because it means she'll make a great vampire. Apollo appears and challenges Smarra to a duel.

LXXXIII.

Charlus! Where are you! I shrieked with my mind,
But like a bat in a void, in return
Nothing echoed. My hatred for mankind
Was aroused. My tongue licked my teeth. The burn
Of the sun told me it was time for a drink,
But then, just as my thirst started to think
For itself, I heard my chimera's voice...
Why not turn her — by force — then and there? Choice...
I hadn't had one — really — but her rage...
I needed to make sure Charlus was safe,
My kidnapped, enslaved, mankind-hating waif —
He would *not* be harmed or locked in a cage!
I heard her say the words: "holy water,"
And chose to turn Vilcor's troubled daughter.

LXXXIV.

She *was* dangerous…Charlus had been right —
And holy water and oil that's been blessed
Are like narcotics for vampires. *He might
Have been drugged and tortured, put to the test,*
I thought, *found out —* I needed an ally —
And with Lucy and Charlus at my side,
And the mambos, priests and bokors all dried
To the bone, then I could approach *her,* try
To turn her heart, make it burn with desire,
Make it feel the thirst of the cursed vampire!
*Lucy, you first, then, there'll be work to do —
We'll drink the priest's blood together, then we'll
Kill your parents, and, if it tries to steal
My chimera, we'll wage war on voodoo*

LXXXV.

Itself! I burst through the great double doors,
And wild-eyed, startled a masked slave. — "Your mask,
Monsieur!" he exclaimed, afraid of my spoors.
I used my sleeve, and was about to ask…
When I heard Lucy's voice softly coming
From an adjoining room. She was humming
To herself. — *Perfect,* I thought, and went in
Sensing that she'd be alone. *Let's begin,
Shall we?* I uttered with my mind, but then
Stopped short in the doorway, surprised to find
She was not alone. Somehow I'd been blind
To her mother's presence. I blinked, but when
I took in her appearance I could see
A brown string at her neck…"Fucking gris-gris,"

LXXXVI.

I muttered, following it to a bulge
Beneath some muslin that covered her chest.
"Pardon me, madame, but would you indulge
Lucy and I – at your husband's request –
To have a word in private?" – "Don't mind me,"
She said. "But should we all move outside?" – "See,"
I spluttered, "I don't believe that's needed
Right at this moment…" And as I kneaded
My words into an argument, that half
Of the room receded, and Lucy's thoughts
Received my urgent cerebral onslaughts.
— *They think I need protecting.* — *Well, don't laugh,*
I did just come in meaning to propose…
— *I know…and my mother already knows.*

LXXXVII.

— *They think they know, but there's much they do not*
About my proposal, and about you…
— *Well, they certainly don't know about thought*
Communicating between minds. I threw
A smile at her mother, some trifling words.
Tell me, do you also talk to the birds?
I mean it! Sometimes I long to be one.
My brother wanted Paris — Me? the sun!
To be a hawk — like a shark in the sky —
But they wouldn't let me become a nun…Why?
They think I'm too corrupt, even for God.
So they want me to get married. How odd…
To trust a man where you question the Lord!
I'm sorry, Just-M., I hope you're not bored —
It's what you get penetrating me here —
A monologue, a captive's stare made clear —
You should know, if we are to be betrothed,

That in this house I'm altogether loathed.
I blamed my fate on Charles and Apollo,
But I never could mourn it, or wallow
In lost innocence, rather…I felt free —
What I mean is when those two came to me
With their masculinities on the line,
Inebriated with perique and wine
Still trying to prove, despite their desire
For each other (having already, prior
To me, failed with slave girls) that they were men.
I had no choice it seemed at first, but then,
Trapped and faced with things I'd wondered about,
I cooperated — One, the lookout
Stood by the door, while the other one tried
To get his member to stay hard inside
Long enough to go in and out…I did
What I could but Apollo's manhood hid
Itself, tucked away in my brother's heart.
Dear Charles, however, practiced in the art
Of punishing slaves, well, he found a way…
The lamentations were loud on the day
I was found, miraculously, with child.
I was, in fact, mercifully exiled
To a convent, but they sent me back home —
My honesty'd called to mind Ancient Rome,
Or something like that, so, back to Belle-Grave!
Where it was stillborn…But then Venus gave
Papa one that lived. He named it Cupid.
It's funny, and all so very stupid.
So, they hate me now and want to pass off
Their depraved wares — Too bad they can't sell me!
— Antigone, if you want to be free,
I said, echoing my words with a cough
To hide my emotion from her mother —
I know a freedom that's like no other…

LXXXVIII.

I was moved, my Lucy came ready-made.
She had lifted herself beyond the pale.
What would she think when I took this charade,
Revealed its working and lifted the veil?
Life is not such a precious thing. I read –
Was it in Lucretius of Rome? – the dead
Know what the living know nothing about:
Pleasure. For even the truly devout
Don't see that the gods have concealed its truth,
Like the tricksters and puppeteers they are –
That life's greatest pleasure is death, by far –
Far beyond love and the vigor of youth –
Death! It's why men fear and desire it so –
Wanting to know what they don't want to know –

LXXXIX.

But you found your body amongst the weeds
Of mankind's written and unwritten laws,
Like a crime, hastily covered with reeds,
Uncovered, reembodied – Now: the claws
The long uncut nails, the wild unkempt hair,
The alabaster skin, the ice cold stare –
They're right: there's no morality there. I –
I am the one who can give you that sky,
To fly above the hands that pull the strings –
I am not a man and I never was,
I am a monster – and despite the peach fuzz,
I brushed my chin, *very old. This mask springs*
Not from life, but through death – The cursed are blessed.
I could sense her heart pounding in her chest.

XC.

*Join me...*I started to say when the door
Opened and Apollo stood there, shaking.
He glanced at me as he said — "Madame, your
Presence has been requested..." (the aching
In my teeth increased) "by Monsieur Labelle."
— "Thank you, Apollo," not moving, she said.
— "He says it's urgent," he added, his head
Held high as he tried, it seemed, to compel
His master's wife to leave the room. — "Please, go,
Mama. He's making me nervous." — "Hello,
Apollo," I said, returning his look.
My teeth sharpened; my lips bulged and grew tight.
Madame Labelle sighed, got up. — "Oh, alright."
But Apollo stayed, and stood there, and shook.

XCI.

Through a palpable silence, Lucy spoke.
— "Why are you still here, Apollo? Just leave — "
— "I will," he said, nodding. "I — " his voice broke.
"I've been reassigned — even as I grieve — "
He choked again, "for Charles — to the fields — So..."
— "They discovered your plot to kill Pap-" — "No!
It's him! He killed Charles! I know it!" I leapt
To my feet. "Look! Where's his mask? Has he kept
To his own prescriptions? No! There are none!
He's a conman! A murderer! A liar!
In a word he's — " — *Lucy, I'm a vampire —*
— "A scoundrel!" — *Join me — Let me make you one —*
— "On my honor!" — "Would you shut up, you fool!"
— "As a MAN, I challenge you to a duel!"

XCII.

— "I accept. Now, be so kind as to share
The when and the where, and then, like she said,
Shut up and leave! We can settle this there."
— "The family plots. There's an oak that's half-dead.
Meet me there, monsieur. I am ready now."
I smiled and watched him, out of habit, bow
To Lucy before storming out the door.
— *Don't worry, his blood will serve to restore*
My complexion. When you see me next I'll —
— *Tell me, what do I have to do? — Just drink...*
Just drink this blood — I slit my wrist — *and sink...*
Her tongue entered the fresh wound like a vile
Worm — *and sink into oblivion...death...*
Then I snapped the bones in her neck mid-breath —

EIGHT

Smarra goes to fight the duel with Apollo, thinking they'll make quick work of it, but one of Apollo's seconds is smoking a cigar made with consecrated incense. This blinds Smarra temporarily. Lucy, now a vampire, appears, having just killed her father. Three zombies show up (Venus, the physician and the condemned slave.) Smarra leaves Lucy to finish off Apollo, and goes to find Minerva in order to turn her.

XCIII.

Dear reader, I'm sure you saw this coming —
My model is famous in his writing
For duels, and eating cherries, and humming
When he was young, some mornings out fighting
Duels over words between boys said in jest.
Mankind has always walked on eggshells lest
Its honor gets triggered, its fraud revealed,
Its baselessness exposed and unconcealed,
When blood must be spilled, a sacrifice made,
To prove its importance, recharge the lie —
I, of course, had nothing to prove, just I
Was thirsty. I'd taken Lucy and laid
Her down on the floor, as though she'd fainted.
Beautiful...just as though she'd been painted.

XCIV.

Well, I *was* upset — not to be downplayed.
Charlus and voodoo circled in my mind.
I was dying of thirst — my nerves were frayed —
But still my senses strained themselves to find
My chimera, a glimpse, a scent, a sound —
Like Pegasus hovering, I felt bound
By her, the Chimaera's, maneuverings,
Even though her flames sought to burn my wings.
What am I if not a monster lover?
And what was Pegasus if not a horse
With wings cutting an unnatural course,
Like my verses, striving to discover
Love in another monster's eyes — descry
Truths in the grist of old myths — from the sky —

XCV.

Soon the half-dead oak tree came into view,
My challenger there, before it, waiting.
In the shadows there stood another two.
I approached, my thirst anticipating
A quick massacre, and said — "There you are!
And Brontes too, holding a case of guns…
I assumed we'd fight with our teeth, like Huns!"
The third man was smoking a strong cigar.
"I'm sorry, Apollo, I came alone.
Neither seconds nor pistols of my own."
Apollo's sleeves were rolled up, his vest tight.
— "Oh? What about — what *was* his name? — Charlus?"
His words wrapped around my throat like a noose —
I leapt into the air and from that height

XCVI.

I meant to fall upon Apollo first —
But as I pounced, a puff of acrid smoke
Swelled into my face like a noxious burst
Of swamp gas, and blinded, as though a cloak
Had been thrown over my head, to the ground
I tumbled — but I heard Apollo scream.
My talons had dug out a bloody stream
From his shoulder to his waist, and that sound
Brought my fingers to my lips and I licked,
Even as they rudely pummeled and kicked
My body, curled up in the soil and dirt,
The man's blood and sucked pieces of his flesh,
Until, as though through a dissolving mesh,
My eyesight returned and I rose unhurt.

XCVII.

Catching one of their legs mid-kick, I bit,
So hard the bone cracked, and the giant fell.
I gorged on his blood thirstily and quit
Only when I heard the other man yell
For help and begin to run, then I leapt
Again through the air, landing on his back.
— "The enchanted smoke man, with his stuffed sack
Of consecrated incense — How inept!"
I gurgled through my hot, bubbling teeth,
Plunging them into the wet flesh beneath
And wrathfully sucked until it was dry.
"So, Apollo...where were we? Oh, that's right..."
He was on one knee. "You still have some fight
In you, I see. Up! But before you die

XCVIII.

'Like a man,' I want you to know the truth.
I have no honor — I am not a man — "
— "I know that," he spat. — "And despite my youth,
I am very old. In fact, my lifespan
Is hard to predict...As long as there's blood..."
Where he knelt, *his* had formed a pad of mud.
"But I digress — Your duel has been in vain.
It's not that you lost, it's that your campaign
To die with honor, to prove your manhood,
Was directed at a creature whose sex
Is not that of a man...Mine was complex,
Rich, diverse, multiple, and if I should
Present myself as masculine today...
Well, there's power in doing it that way.

XCIX.

But I'd never betray the truth inside:
To prove I'm not a monster, *rape a girl*,
To prove that I'm a man, fight a duel, hide
My shame (if I had any) in the whirl
Of insecurities passed down as strengths —
But you, Apollo, have gone to great lengths
To deserve those superficial titles:
'Free,' 'white,' 'virile' — Spare me the recitals!
'Man', in a word, *'Time's puppet'*, unaware
And immoral, fictitious and cruel!" — "Sir..."
— "Not 'sir!'" I stripped off my shirt. "Do not err
Again!" and my breasts, exposed to the air,
Rose like scythes, upturned. — "We should have never
Done that to Lucy, I..." — "Oh, whatever!"

C.

My eyes aflame turned to Lucy's delight.
She smiled as though waking up from sound sleep.
She was drenched in blood, "My hair is affright,
I'm sure. Oh, I left Papa in a heap
On the drawing room floor—The others though...
They got away." —"Lucy...are you sick?" —"No!
It's the world that's sick, Apollo. *I'm well!*"
She laughed, as though incredulous. —"What hell
Is this?" —"It's true, we are the afterlife,
"In a sense..." I began, when we heard moans
From the gravesites nearby, as though the bones
Of Lucy's ancestors had come to life
And began to make noise. —"Hello, Venus!"
(Of course, she had joined the zombie genus.)

CI.

—"She's a zombie, Lucy." —"Oh, and them too?"
The doctor stumbled behind her, followed
Close by by Charlus's powdered slave. —"Who?"
Apollo twisted around and swallowed
Hard on his pain and confusion. —"But *where*,"
I demanded, grabbing him by the hair,
"Is Charlus?" my nails digging into his chest.
He panted, —"Miss- Miss-" but I knew the rest.
—"Lucy, finish him, and...avoid *them*, I—
I have to find Charlus—" I couldn't wait
For her because...it wasn't true. Debate
Amongst yourselves, dear readers, whether my
Chimerical obsession was folly,
Sounding the depths of my melancholy,

CII.

But I had to face Minerva alone.
She was my Chimaera. I know it's strange —
And in the next chapter I'll try to own
This myth that I've found it fitting to change.
For now, let me say, my chimera had
Begun to recall an ideal gone mad —
From chimera to *Chimaerical* beast —
The illusion had been unchained, released —
I'd seen power in the sharp openings
Of her eyes, but I'd not perceived the threat
(An oversight I had come to regret)
Those openings posed to my beating wings...
But still, though before her, I was exposed,
I longed to see that her eyes never closed.

NINE

Smarra rampages back to the plantation house, kills a priest sent for Charles's funeral, finds Madame Labelle hiding under a piece of furniture and offers to kill her for Minerva. Minerva orders Smarra to let Madame Labelle go and engages with them. Smarra tries to convince Minerva to become a vampire, while Minerva distracts them until someone sneaks up and, using a medical syringe, injects them with holy water.

CIII.

I sensed people fleeing, taking cover
As I blew through the courtyard towards the house.
I found it comical to discover
A brave soul at the door, ready to douse
My head with water, but before he could
Cross himself, I grabbed his hands where he stood,
Tore them off and licked my lips in the spray —
Then I tossed his head through the entrance way.
— *"Priests,"* I grumbled, threshing through the front
door.
"Minerva!" I cried. "High queen of voodoo…
Come out! I have a proposal for you.
And no more fucking incense, and no more
Priests — Just you — Be brave — You know how I feel —
Look — *topless* — I have nothing to conceal —

CIV.

Except my tail—I can show you that, too,
If you like…" Just then I heard something move—
Something hiding behind a chair…one shoe…
"I don't mean to scare, I mean to improve…"
Protruding…"Why, *bonsoir*, Madame Labelle!"
I grabbed her foot and pulled the woman out.
"Minerva, I got you a gift! Devout,
Stupid, prejudiced, slave-owning and, well,
Your owner! Come out and free yourself! Here!"
I shook her violently and she wailed. "Fear,
Madame. Fear and confusion *taste so sweet!*"
I shook her again. —"Let her go, mister."
I shuddered. "Let her go. She's my sister."
—"Sissy!" she howled from her knees at my feet.

CV.

"Help me!" Then *she* appeared…and I was crushed
By her beauty—My hands went limp in awe—
Madame Labelle fled as my forehead flushed,
And my teeth withdrew back into my jaw—
—"Forgive me, I meant to present Vilcor…"
I said trailing off. She was even more
Beautiful than the night before…Her lips
And her eyes were sharp as razors, their tips
Turned down: the very portrait of disdain.
I longed to hold her up—alive, undead—
With her piercing eyes—a medusa's head
Capturing mankind's confusion and pain
In momentary masks of brutal art—
Before the rest of us tore them apart—

CVI.

"But Lucy laid claim to her father's blood.
Like Pegasus, I had meant to buck him,
Bellerophon/Vilcor, and with a thud
At your feet, you'd be free…free to suck *him*
Dry, for a change…Please, remove that gris-gris…
I have plans I'd like to share *privately*…"
She clutched the bag tightly around her neck
And laughed. Her mind was closed. I felt the check
Like a prison door. "These slavers will fall
If I have my way — Join me — You will rule
From the shadows until times change, then you'll
Emerge one day — not a day older. All
This could be yours! You're like me — We're the same!
Monstrous, in each other's eyes, and aflame!"

CVII.

And so what, dear reader, if I've
Forced this myth, turned it, even, upside down!
I'm a poet, and, qua poet, survive
On traditions whose lifeblood is renown
For its symbols and themes, its *formes fixes* –
Passed down through the arts from the ancient Greeks –
And in my art the Chimaera unlives –
And the sonnet stanza itself still gives
Life to my fantasies, memories, my
Chimeras, the lights that flash in my skies,
As I crash against truths and clash with lies
Daily and nightly and will till I die,
Creating statues, like Medusa's son,
Monuments against time's oblivion.

CVIII.

"You sound just like him — Vilcor — with his myths,
Giving us all these ridiculous names;
From the fieldhands, to the cooks, to the smiths,
No choice, but to play along with his games.
And now, with Lucy's insistent new friend,
What games will...they introduce in the end?
Mama warned me to never sell my soul —
Not for freedom, not even for control —
Not when the devil walks through your front door — "
— "Or your master's?" Her expression was calm.
Her fearlessness worked on me like a balm.
She's defiant, not afraid, at her core.
She could embrace, even come to desire
The inhumanity of the vampire...

CIX.

"Where there is mystery, there is evil,"
My foothold held, in the space of her breath,
"It's been thought by some, but their medieval
Reaction is merely the fear of death.
Remove the fears, and the shadows come clear.
And what is life but time, getting older?
Anxiously getting colder and colder,
Until the warmth of the shroud gets so near
To your thoughts that you can't wait for its gauze
To wrap up your mortal skin and its flaws?
But die *now* and the eternal beyond
Will be your fountain of eternal youth —
Beyond good and evil, falsehood and truth —
Forever from mankind's hold vagabond!"

CX.

—"What do you want from me, *Chauve-souris*?"[3]
—"I want you to join me—to drink my blood—"
She burst out laughing. "I want us to be
Two heads of the same monster—the same flood
That periodically engulfs the land—"
Just then I heard a baby's cry and fanned
Out my senses when I felt a sharp prick
In my back—Her question had been a trick
To distract me! "The goat without horns..." —"Oh?
"You know about that then?" —"Where is Charlus?"
She spat. From my eyes, nose and ears profuse
Streams of blood began to purge out and flow—
And as I collapsed, I glimpsed in the dust
The syringe they'd use to make me combust.

---

[3] "Bat" (French)

69

TEN

Smarra is delirious and, in a dream, recounts meeting the vampire who turned them. Smarra, presenting as a woman, a witch, during the medieval period, gathers together a race of pagans, disaffected youth and criminals, who kill priests and generally attack Christendom. One night before the massacre of a seminary, Smarra hears their maker's voice and is drawn away. He explains why he turned them (their hermaphroditism seemed like a beautiful representation of nature's diversity), but regrets having turned them into a monster. He then tells the story of how he was turned. Smarra wakes up to find a voodoo ritual being led by Minerva, who is about to sacrifice Cupid. Smarra is able to get to Cupid first, which reinvigorates them. They kill everyone they can, but leave Minerva lying on the ground close to death.

CXI.

You can guess what they'd put in that syringe —
But I took comfort in the fleeting thought
Of a headless, handless priest at the hinge
Of a swinging door — Still my mind was fraught
With memories and dreams, nightmares, bad things —
So my comfort was short-lived — I heard songs
From my village, my mother's voice, screams, wrongs
Committed, the panic, the clamorings
Of war, and I saw my whole village burned…
I went as a woman when I first turned.
A witch back then was not without power.
I only turned pagans, disaffected
Youths and others already infected
With a criminal need to devour…

CXII.

"Priest-Eaters," they called us — A strange new race —
Priests were found dead, mutilated, sucked dry —
A counter-crusade that has left no trace
In the narratives propagated by
The Christians. A great seminary stood
Near a copse that had been a sacred wood —
As if we needed an extra excuse!
We all had our histories of abuse,
And most had chosen to die on the oath
That they'd be reborn with a monstrous thirst
To drink the blood of the hypocrites first,
Then man's every other diseased outgrowth —
But the night of the massacre, a voice
Reached me and I felt like I had no choice...

CXIII.

It was my maker's voice. Somehow I knew,
Though I hadn't seen him since he'd saved me.
I had to go. Quietly, I withdrew,
And found him concealed behind an old tree.
He wore the monk's robes, and his hair was shorn.
Out of habit, my mind flooded with scorn —
Then he embraced me and pressed me in close —
— "You are beautiful," he said. "Bellicose,
But beautiful...My tragic Medea
Spirited away — The land of the sun
Would mourn you if it had not been undone
By mankind — The world has no idea —
I pray, not to Jesus, but to myself,
That one day it will immolate itself — "

CXIV.

—"You pray, while we burn it all to the ground!"
—"Your fury—it warms that immortal part
Of my monstrous being—Your friends' minds resound
With hatred and the thirst for blood—My heart
Convulses to your horde's combined bloodlust.
It's cold, but still it contracts with desire,
Despite my disguise, I am a vampire
Afterall. Corinth, long since turned to dust,
Was where I was made…dead—undead—alive—
What are we, child? For now, we just survive—
Invisible leeches or parasites—
I was a pagan, I'm now one of them.
Speaking fluent Latin, at least, pro tem.
My days are filled with chanting, but my nights…"

CXV.

My eyes flashed open, my teeth gnashed, I clenched—
I was being carried, but when I tried
To struggle free, something burned me, I flinched—
And as the drug surged and then creeped inside,
I succumbed again to dreams of the past—
I was telling him—speaking very fast—
—"Join us—Help us destroy Christendom—They
Will not stop until it's destroyed—That day,
You saved me, now let me save you—Come out!
Join our family—Warm your heart—Slake your thirst
On the blood of the oppressors—!" —"First—*First*—"
He gently urged, "Let me tell you about
That day…" He held my arm, *my attention*,
Without my grasping his real intention—

CXVI.

He spoke slowly, "That day, I was surprised
By a vision. Reality comes through
In visions of truth and beauty disguised
Sometimes. That's what I saw, when I saw you —
Nature in its true and beautiful form —
Multiform and diverse, flooding the banks
Of mankind's categories — 'It outflanks
Reason — I must protect it from this storm
Of fire and ignorance — I must save...them —
The rules of this narrow age would condemn
Nature itself to sacramental pyres — '
But not I, no, not, even if it took
Something equally wrong...So, I forsook
Nature for the unnatural...Vampires...

CXVII.

Vampires, that's what we are, not pagan beasts
Baring the truth of nature's manifold,
As you were: 'male,' 'female,' 'animal' — Priests
See nothing but pure white/pure black, and hold
The rainbow before their eyes in contempt...
But we are monsters now, as yet undreamt
Of by most and still creatures of the night.
Trust me, it's safer to hide than to fight —
Stay — Let me tell you — The one that turned me,
She was my betrothed, until, converted
By her family to Christ, and perverted
By grief and confusion she died, only —
Only to come back one of the undead —
I could have lived...I followed her instead —

CXVIII.

I thought: *We may be cursed, but at least we're* —
Let me finish — *at least we're together* —
Forever, unable to die! That fear
Had been lifted through death, and the tether
To the world as we knew it had snapped — but
That world had not forgotten...We were found...
Somehow I escaped...She was caught and bound...
The horrific cries they caused with each cut...
They knew how to kill her..." — *Something's not right...
I hear screaming...* — "How long have I been here?" —
"Stay!
Stay! They'll kill you too!" — "No! No! Get away — "
And I ran till I saw the pyres alight
With my friends, all my family, dead again...
He'd saved me, betrayed me again, but when

CXIX.

I tried to go to them, my mind awoke —
My tongue licked outside my lips for the blood
I'd vomited. I saw the half-dead oak
And beneath it two heaps crouched in the mud —
— "Quick! It's waking up! Put it down and tie
Its limbs!" I heard, and then a baby's cry —
— "No! Just cut off its head now!" someone wailed.
I kicked and tried to roar and as I flailed
I caught someone's foot and sank my teeth in —
There was screaming and struggling as I sucked —
Someone pulled while my host desperately bucked —
Then I heard Minerva's voice through the din.
— "Bring me the white child!" she yelled. Then, the drums,
The sound that human skin makes when it hums

CXX.

Stretched out over hollowed out wooden bowls —
There was smoke in the air, chanting and prayers —
People were dancing barefoot on hot coals —
She prayed, *"Blanc Dani, Grand Zombi, who dares*
Invoke your powers on this random night?
Minerva Labelle, but you know my truth —
Born to your servant, even in my youth
I sacrificed to you — Now, by the light
Of this moon, accept this cabrit sans cor!
And infuse these strengthening fires with your
Omnipotence, reduce these monstrous things,
These three vampires, twa sa yo chòvsourits[4]
To ash!" But I had gotten myself free,
And got to Cupid first, and with his springs

CXXI.

Of fresh blood, I regained all my forces.
No, I don't believe in *chèvres sans cornes*,
But a baby's blood, as its warmth courses
Through a vampire's veins, makes them feel reborn!
The first thing I did with my strength renewed
Was kiss my chimera against her will,
Deep inside her neck, though I didn't kill
Her, and left her unconscious, neck half-chewed,
My blood smeared hastily over her lips.
Like an icy chill that suddenly whips
Up your spine those two heaps leapt to mind —
They were on fire now, Lucy and Charlus —
I tried to save them, but it was no use —
Mutilated, before they'd been consigned

---

[4] "these three bats" (Haitian Creole)

CXXII.

To the flames, they were headless, de-hearted —
And in their separated hearts a stake
Impaled all hopes of them being restarted —
Still, I begged them, with fresh blood, to awake!
Lucy had bite marks, chunks of flesh missing —
Zombies...and I'd left her there, dismissing
The threat that Charlus tried to make me see —
I could hear my chimera's wheezing plea:
— "Don't kill me — Don't kill me — Don't let me die — "
My blood was in her system and she knew
How close she was to the edge, just a few
Missed breaths and she'd fall into my arms — I
Straddled her, I was naked, I'd been stripped,
Forced more blood on her and watched as it dripped

CXXIII.

Down the side of her mouth. — "You're better off!
Goodness, morality, these are just dreams,
But monstrosity," (she began to cough)
Monstrosity is real. I know it seems
As though we vampires, chòvsourits,[5] we bats
Are the nightmares — in fact, we do not haunt
Your world — It's yourselves, your blind spots, that taunt
You from the dark corners." She convulsed. "That's
What I'm freeing you from: servitude, fear..."
— "We're...not...the...same..." she repeated, eyes wide
Open to the smoke-filled night air, her pride
In her living self undiminished...Here
Is where this episode ends. I left her
Where she lay, and in a chaotic blur

---

[5] "bats" (Haitian Creole)

77

CXXIV.

I spun out into the dark night, unsure
Of where I was going or who I was —
Beyond good and evil, the pure, impure?
Just another fool, like Vilcor, because...?
Well, I could go on spinning out verses,
Depicting new, rehashing old curses,
Tracing the gain and the loss of control,
Bemoaning the dark night of a dark soul,
But I'd rather respect my poem's true end —
I hadn't been able to turn her mind
Before her nature turned against mankind —
Minerva would not be reborn a friend...
At odds with herself, what kind of vampire
Would awake, its throat parched, its eyes on fire...?

Appendix: Pegasus in Love

Our chimeras are what resemble us most.

Victor Hugo

The Young Pegasus

The Death of Perseus

Perseus is turned to stone by Medusa, who is pregnant with Pegasus.

When Perseus opened the gorgon's door,
With Zeus as his father, and at his side
Athena and Hermes, the master guide,
He held a hooked sword, a shield, and wore

Shoes with wings on them, as he meant to soar
Away a hero; but, stone-struck, he died.
From her grotesque beauty he could hide
His stare, and stood there, earthbound to the floor.

Medusa's eyes flared, snakes hissed, then she laughed,
Crossed the entrance hall and, untouched, unvexed,
Closed the door behind him, against the draught.

What was she doing? What should she do next?
She looked at the statue, picked at her scales,
Smiled at the hooves kicking at her entrails —

The Birth of Pegasus

*With Perseus having been killed by Medusa, Pegasus is born
naturally (instead of bursting forth from his mother's severed
neck). Still, Medusa dies in childbirth.*

His dark eyes fluttered after first he fell —
To gasps — from the bed, hard onto the floor.
He kicked, tried to stand, slipped, again he bore,
In the gore he'd made his mother expel,

His weight, down, groundwards, in gross parallel
To her insides, poured out, scraped from the core
Of Poseidon's latest victim. Before,
Though, her eyes could forever flee this hell

Of pain and last thoughts of death and of rape,
Something more reined in her tormented flight —
She saw *wings*: bent, flapping, trailing — The sight

Pried open her eyes, made her fanged maw gape —
But, draped on her body, her snakes were slack,
And before their eyes met, her eyes went black.

The Death of Andromeda

Perseus, having been killed, is not there to save Andromeda from her fate, which she indignantly accepts, accusing her parents of selfishness, preferring to die. The young Pegasus, by himself, observes the scene.

"If it weren't for these chains, O monstrous sea
You'd feel me already beneath the tide —
I'd come to you, slip off this rock and slide
In, like a serpent, disappear and be

A piece of your multiplicity — flee
The commands of mankind and the gods — bride
Now — now sacrifice — *'Be noble and hide
Your fears, your tears, your laughter'* — Ha! but see,

I'm exposed, Sea Monster! Let's make a scene!
I'm through with *you, father — mother — king — queen*!
Now watch the future of your world go down!"

When, over the waves — the sound of thunder —
A foal with spread wings, all awe and wonder,
Beheld Andromeda, yearning to drown.

At the Fountain of Pirene

Pegasus at the Fountain of Pirene

Pegasus comes to drink at the Fountain of Pirene, once a nymph, who was turned into a spring over grief for her son when he died. She too, like Medusa, had been raped by Poseidon.

When Pegasus drank at the weeping pool
Of Pirene, still moving with her tears,
He'd hear her the way a child overhears,
And drink more slowly, his thirst overrule.

This nymph had been raped too, plucked from her school.
Krill, like his mother, to Poseidon's leers.
Ears cocked as he sipped, he'd think how the years
Had cleared these waters of her snot and drool.

*Medusa's son, you have your mother's eyes,
Her multiplicity lives on in you –
My son was killed, and my grief never dies*

*They treat me like a god – I guess it's true –
My future was taken from me, my child...
And the pain...well...even Time was beguiled –*

Bellerophon Meets Medusa's Son at the Fountain of Pirene

Bellerophon comes looking for Pegasus at the Fountain of Pirene to use him in his heroic feats. He thinks he sees Medusa's eyes in the horse, and fears that he'll be turned to stone.

When Pegasus saw Bellerophon, he
Leapt into the air and let his wings fan
Out to their full and terrifying span —
His nostrils, like craters, smoked and debris

Expelled when he snorted, like venom. *Flee* —
Thought Bellerophon, but before he ran
He saw himself mirrored in the dark scan
Of a black stare — He froze — petrified — *"She* —

"She's alive — " he started — stuttered out fast,
Words that, he was certain, would be his last,
For it struck him, at the door of demise:

What had she — Medusa — what had she bred?
For wide and black on the sides of its head
The beautiful beast had its mother's eyes —

The Sons of Poseidon

Bellerophon, who believes he is also one of Poseidon's sons,
exhorts Pegasus to kill the Chimaera in order to earn a place in
Olympus and become a god.

i.

They say it has three heads — but it's a *she*,
So, we won't be outnumbered — She can't fly —
What chance does she have? — She's going to die —
Hear that, Chimaera — easy bitch! — you'll see!

Just like our father did our mothers, *we*
Will do you with this spear thrust from the sky!
And your last twitches, your wet, smoky cry,
Coughing and choking, will herald the free

Entrance into the great hall of the gods
Of Bellerophon and Pegasus — Heirs
To Mount Olympus — Heroes — Monster Slayers —

I can see our father — he smiles and nods —
He approves — to see us chase down this fight —
This monstrosity's ours, brother, *our* right —

ii.

The gods, Pegasus, are with us, I know.
Punishments are prizes—Just are the fates!
Sons of the Horse God—*us*, brother—Let's go!
The doors may be locked but the gargoyle waits—

I admit a desire to see her blow
Her fire from three heads—to see which one mates
Best with my spear—its lead—Fly close, I'll throw—
Choke her—turn the key—one-two-three, then *gates*

Apotheotic will open, my friend!
Olympus will greet us, this exile end!
Our father despotic will show us in!

This is our chance, the heavens are right there—
Up past the clouds, through the sky, through the air—
The ichor will glow that flows in this skin!

The Death of Bellerophon

i.

Bellerophon misses, failing to kill the Chimaera with his lead-tipped spear, but when he tries to flee, Pegasus brings him back and bucks him so that he lands before the Chimaera.

The flames she breathed had licked his shoe leather
When his spear nicked her side and skipped away —
She roared — hissed — her goat-head yelled in dismay
When he surged upwards and like a feather

Danced in the air, as though on a tether
Taunting her — for Pegasus, in her sway,
Could not stop looking, and choosing to stay,
Made Bellerophon — again — altogether —

Face the Chimaera's cacophonous three —
Each one an open mouth venting its glee —
When, bucked off, he fell right there before her.

Pegasus relished his gift to the beast.
Hooves set to ground shyly near the horror,
He heard the man's screams and witnessed the feast —

ii.

Meditation on Pegasus as a symbol for art, and the meaning of
monstrosity.

If Pegasus were real and something more
Than poetry, than a symbol for art,
Used to overcome nature and depart
For the heavens — used by poets to soar —

He'd have bucked Bellerophon long before
He felt the sharp spurs of his counterpart,
And cringed at the cry of the young upstart
Who thought he could storm mortality's door —

For reflected in the Chimaera's eyes
Six times Pegasus would have seen the rise
And fall of his wings flapping in the air —

And the monster seen, the multiple beast,
He'd have bucked his charge and served up a feast
Of madman, for *them, têtes-à-tête*, to share —

iii.

For too many years I've lived in a dream
Drowning in false ideals and on fire—
Afraid to move, fool enough to aspire
To flights my heart would then deem too extreme—

But madly I believed. My self-esteem
Weighted with pride, would drive on my desire
Like a team of winged horses—I'd cry, "Higher!"
Wheezing into the thin air and thick steam

Of a mirage—then, in a heap of shame,
I wouldn't even remember the name
Of the chimera that had led me there—

Like a Bellerophon, dazed and confused,
Lost in a wasteland, embarrassed but used
To Pegasus bucking me in midair—

The Children of Echidna

*"And she conceived and bore
offspring...Orthrus...Cerberus...the Hydra of Lerna...who
Heracles slew...and the Chimaera, who breathed fire...who
was three-headed... lion...goat...serpent...who was killed by
noble Bellerophon, riding Pegasus."*

Theogony. Hesiod

Heracles

The Monster Slayer (the Nemean Lion)

*Heracles describes being driven mad by Hera to kill his sons,
his material future, and how he then came to realize that any
future he might have lay in becoming a god (apotheosis). He
kills the Nemean Lion, whose skin he will wear, and offers the
rest to the gods.*

Heroes are not born, no, they are made,
And Hera made me when she drove me mad —
She made me snuff out the future I had —
They trembled before me, my sons, afraid —

I was wild, my hands were like cat claws splayed —
"Please father," my eldest tried hard to say,
His brother behind his legs hid, then they
Died torn apart — but, my future betrayed,

I knew there could be another — I prayed:
How much for a place near the Pleiad?
I wasn't given a number, but clad
Soon enough in a lionskin I'd flayed,

The naked carcass of its monster laid
At the feet of the gods: *There! I will pay*
For my star with these — Hear me! I will slay
As many as it takes, until I've paid! —

The Lernaean Hydra

Heracles describes killing the Lernaean Hydra, and calculates
how much its many heads should have been worth.

I learned my lesson the hard way — I mean:
To apotheosis, there are no short
Cuts. I pursued the Hydra's whole cohort,
But all those snake heads were only a screen

For one shrieking head, monstrous and obscene,
At the center, that, at last, I scooped out —
I counted hundreds, but the gods throughout
Countered my many with one serpentine

Being, one kill, to the counter one bean —
Never mind that from each head's severed port
Another two would spring, writhe and contort!
I had to learn to abort them between

Prunings — Eventually a routine
Of cut off and sear before they could sprout
Was found…Still, she had the — without a doubt —
Most multiples of "1" I've ever seen…

Orthrus

Heracles describes killing Orthrus, the two-headed dog, father of the Nemean Lion.

I killed a two-headed dog — I was told
That my lionskin belonged to his son —
He'd had two whelps with his sister, and one
Was sacrificed, by me, processed and sold

To the gods in exchange for rays of gold,
To be paid in full at my journey's end,
When up into the night sky I ascend
And in eternity gain my foothold —

"Here, boy," I whistled, "Come here…" but the old
Cur climbed some rocks — He'd already begun
To sense my intentions, and so to run —
Or so I thought — when he pounced! *Very bold!*

I thought — He was on me — We kicked and rolled —
I had one neck I was trying to rend,
When the other bit the lion's skin…"Send
My regards to you kid —" I roared, "twofold!"

Cerberus

Heracles describes when he captured Cerberus to bring him back up to the living. He briefly considers attempting to rescue his family from death instead.

The three-headed dog, though, I didn't kill.
I was told to bring it up from the dead —
The thought crossed my mind that maybe instead
Like Asclepius (strength in place of skill)

I could bring back my wife, children, and still
Have a future, but then, it was so dark
Down there, and I thought what's a patriarch
Compared to a star? What's anything? *Nil.*

Nothing can compare to that kind of thrill —
Eternal fame, my name written, sung, said
By overawed onlookers, overhead
My constellation forever unstill —

Lost in thought now, I couldn't wait until
My mortal life was over — *Hark! The stark
Hiss of its tail, the triple bark-bark-bark!
Destiny calls,* I thought, racing downhill!

Bellerophon

The Chimaera

A description of Bellerophon being bucked by Pegasus and devoured by the Chimaera.

And what if the Chimaera does not die,
But is saved by a horse with flapping wings,
Who finds his voice and as a monster sings
To her a song, lustfully, from the sky —

We would audibly hear Pegasus sigh,
When Bellerophon cries: *Behold the beast!*
And before the lead-tipped lance is released
See Bellerophon fall, bucked early: *Why!*

He cries now, but then, crashing down nearby,
Moans as her lionhead tears apart — flings
His broken body and life away — Rings
Of intestine horrify, beautify

The scene! The air's sprayed with bloody pink dye!
And his love for her like a fire's increased —
Maybe she invites him to join the feast —
He alights, and she tosses him a thigh —

Ode to the Chimaera

i.

Three heads and three breaths
　　　　and three pairs of eyes
the same name: *nature*
　　　　in its multiple
truth: *monstrosity* –

　　　　Everyone fears you!

and even the gods
　　　　hurl men at your flames
like Bellerophon,
　　　　who came seeking fame,
apotheosis
　　　　and a father's love –

but Pegasus came
　　　　with his mother's eyes,
always to have you,
　　　　the Chimaera, in
stone, chimerical –

ii.

        Floating in between

earth and the heavens

        a horse born with wings,

a being at odds,

        a monster tending

upwards to the gods

he could not outfly

        the reach of your flames,

and inspired sang:

"As high as your eyes

        can see, no higher!

As high as your eyes

        can see, that's how high!

for reflected I

        see myself six times

sent up from below

        a winged horse on fire —

and I'd rather burn!"

OTHER DARK POEMS

Alexandrines in Lafayette Cemetery

I walked along the wall
>of the house of the dead,

And ferns stuck their fingers
>out to welcome me in.

I entered by the gates
>that read "Lafayette." Old,

Old air came near me and
>said, *Bonsoir, mon amour…*

Have you come back to me?
>*Yes…How could you forget?*

I was your first mistress,
>*your first love, your first sin.*

When you left me I died
>*and since then I have been*

Here…My heart is unchanged,
>*My heart still beats for you.*

My breath still breathes, these lips
>*that refused your adieu*

Burn for you still…Over
>the tombs and in the trees

I could hear the wind blow
                    and I recalled the sea,

The storms and the scars all
                    came back to me, the world

That betrays...endlessly,
                    all the false ports, the weighs

Of anchor...*I'm ready,*
                    I said, *this time to stay* —

An old, old air took me
                    And, yes, led me astray,

Into a room buried
                    in the house of the dead —

And now in the stillness
                    I sense, sometimes I feel,

The walls shake and crack and
                    the ferns through the
stone...They're

Welcoming the storm-tossed
                    and the tired back home...

The Vampire

I

Dreams of Decadence

It's not so much a coffin, where I sleep
But a bath where I do not doze, I steep
Thinking and scheming and plotting a drink
Submerging and letting all my thoughts sink
     into a pool of blood…

     …and, in my dreams, the flood
Fills my mouth and my throat, and warms my skin
Like wine, once upon a time, from within
Until half-mad and excited with thirst
I stir, cadaverous, starved and accursed –

II

Tears of Wine

The blood in my glass looks like chocolate wine.
The film inside creeps down like long fingers,
Shadows on the wall, the shame that lingers
From the night before, both foul and fine

In the moonlight — They want it, and I laugh.
Children — no — pets, cattle, blood bags that calve
More wineskins, you want what you cannot have...
The check for this drink is your epitaph!

Still, they stare, they watch it swell at my lips!
I am beautiful, and desire craves
The forbidden not in sips, but in waves
Till it burns like poison, courses and rips —

Come...Don't just taste the unknown with your eyes —
Have a sip, but not from my glass, try this...
And when you wake up, remember whose kiss
Made you an undead distiller of cries.

III

Self-Portrait in a Still Life

I am a plucked rose in a vase of blood,
A still life in a frame and beyond time,
A dead piece of nature in meter and rhyme
I soak up eternity in a flood

Of dead men and women, the vital mud
This flower needs to enrich its sublime
And singular beauty; forever, I'm
One futureless bloom, not a single bud —

And if on occasion I nick the vein
That surges down a ridged cock when it's thick,
Or pierce with my fangs lips I tease and lick,

It's not for the sex, but for the warm spurt
In my mouth — of ecstasy — as I drain
Their bodies, and leave them dry and inert.

IV

Danse Macabre — Desiccated Extremity

You'll want to see it, but will fade to black
    Before your desire can have its way —
At the touch, through my clothes, you'll start, pull back
    But swept up in my swift waltz of dismay

You'll succumb, unsatisfied and the lack
    Will haunt your visions slowly sucked away
Where confused, maybe you'll blame the cognac,
    Then writhe in my arms, then lilt and then
sway —

    The thing you died wanting was old and dried,
Desiccated into a hairy root —
It putrefied first, like a rotting fruit;

    But vampires, when they die as women, hide
Wilted black petals that keep their perfume,
Impregnating their tomb's still, stale vacuum —

V

Sonnet

I have no regrets, my immortal ways
Suit me and I miss nothing of the past;
My future's an eternal present, stays
Like a dream, untimed, my days and nights last

Forever, untouched by the hours' haste.
Slow, they are decadent, I take my time,
Pleasure when squandered is the only waste
I know, to me, mortality's a crime.

But that doesn't mean I don't sometimes feel,
Out of boredom if not some other need,
A longing for something new and unreal
Calling me forth to create, intercede

And (proud of the things I have and will sire)
Abort nature with a newborn vampire.

Goethe Contemplating the Composition of "The Bride of Corinth"

The poet, with his penetrating stare
Breaking forth from beneath his low, dark brow
With the vehemence of caged light somehow
Released, pondered something that was not there —

The room was empty, motes danced in the air,
But in him something stirred...Would he allow
It to exist? Or...would he disavow
The pagan monster, whispering, *Beware*

The Christian cult — Use your talent and breath
To sing me *into existence: my death*
From grief, my return, brought back by desire

For the heathen to whom I'd been betrothed...
Before converting to a faith I loathed!
Compose your ballad...for the first vampire!

The Mares

But surely the madness of mares surpasses all.
Georgics. Virgil

Visions at the Death of Glaucus

Glaucus, who refused to allow his racing mares to mate, is
killed by them during a chariot race.

When Glaucus refused her his virgin mares
To create a more than natural speed,
Aphrodite conceived in them a need
Before all the cries and onlookers' stares

To eat him alive. His two racing pairs
First bucked and reared, then turned their mad
stampede,
The quadriga flipped, then steed over steed
They bounded — four frenzied maenadic hares —

For their maker — tall, hubristic, cocksure.
In their movements — lithe, excessive, impure —
We saw the goddess appear at his fall…

We all shared one breath, devout and afraid
When over the beasts — sleek with blood and gall —
There pranced stout Pegasus high on parade —

The Mares of Diomedes, Hercules and the Dead

Hercules, having captured Diomedes' mares, who had been raised to feed on human flesh, comes to find that they have eaten his friend Abduras.

As Hercules watched the monstrous mares gnash
On the shreds of flesh and the shards of bone
Still caught in their teeth, and saw the earth sown
With his friend's remains — a mess there to mash

And mud-pulp under hoof — from grief a flash
Of guilt filled his eyes: *I left him alone.*
Now for Abduras there escaped a groan
And then a regret: "Diomedes, *rash*

I was to kill you, when your beasts want more.
Well, lucky for them the harvest was rich
And I am lavish with the spoils of war.

Here, ladies, your master's corpse — It's still warm —
You won't hear his scream, but his limbs might twitch —
Come, eat him up quick, before the flies swarm — "

Leimone, the Horse-Maiden

*Imprisoned for losing her virginity before marriage, Leimone
addresses the starving mare meant to eat her alive as
punishment.*

Mares of Glaucus and Diomedes' mares,
Mares of evil, like you, the mares of men —
Virgins plucked, broken in, debauched and then
Tamed into brutal but usable wares —

Your heartless eyes reflect in mine like flares —
Look — We're both monsters enclosed in this pen —
They hate us and fear us, those men, but when
We're free we'll show them who claims us as heirs:

Medusa-Centaur! And awful before
Hands raised and pleading, disavowing, pale —
We'll show no mercy — slaughter every male!

And when Mankind kneeling in its own gore
Asks, "Who are you?" We'll laugh. "Just a girl named
Leimone and a mare that she untamed!"

Three Bulls

The Rape of Europa

"If the boys here bore you, why don't you mate
With him?" her friends had joked. "Europa, see —
"He likes you!" and laughed when, knee next to knee,
It knelt down before her and seemed to wait.

She'd shrugged, approached cautiously, took the bait —
"Hello," she said as she climbed on when he
Rose suddenly, and then made for the sea —
She'd called, but already it was too late...

Beneath the immortal weight of the bull
She'd prayed to the god Thanatos to pull
Her soul from her body, but went unheard —

She knew that it was no use and unwise —
For she'd recognized Zeus, when from its eyes
The god's lightning had flashed without a word —

Pasiphae's Bull

The bull had raced past her, paused, turned its head —
Had it seen her? — then it galloped away —
The mad bull of Crete — It's beautiful — "Stay!"
But it hadn't stayed and away it sped —

"I stood out, LIKE A GODDESS, but instead
Of liking my beauty, to my dismay
He looked right through me — and, what can I say?
I'm a woman, he's a bull...Oh," she said,

"Daedalus, what can you do?" So, he thought
For a day, and, in a week, there it stood...
She climbed in and pressed her ass to the wood —

With fresh menstrual blood from a cow — still hot —
He painted the hole and Pasiphae's cunt —
Then they hid (each proud of their godlike stunt) —

Ariadne's Brother

*Ariadne waits, unsure if it will be Theseus or the Minotaur
who will emerge from the labyrinth.*

Crouched in the shadows by the labyrinth door —
The night watch having abandoned its post —
Tricked into thinking they had seen a ghost —
Ariadne listened and heard a roar —

She smiled, but…to celebrate before
She knew for sure…Would it be *guest* or *host*?
Who would she need to be ready to toast?
Victory or Release? Theseus or —

Suddenly the door seemed to shake with rage —
She sprang to her feet and with all her weight
Pulled — and rejoiced when, unable to wait,

Expelling dust and darkness from its cage,
She saw her brother's snout push through the crack —
The hero's fresh blood dripping hot and black —

Mankind's Spider

after Denis Villeneuve's Enemy
and Gustave Doré's Arachne

A brown sun rises in a smog-stained sky
The day breaks in a bleak and somber way;
As he starts to leave, she begs him to stay —
He turns on her, in horror, asks her why:

"Is your bed a web, Mistress? Did I lie
In sheets edged with Arachne's twisted fray?
I recall two legs begging me to play,
Were there more? Like Doré's? Three from each thigh?"

He grabs his shoe and slams it on the ground,
"Die, Spider!" he laughs and throws back his head —
But when he comes to, her eight legs are spread —

And frozen, sick to his stomach with dread
He thinks he should turn and run but instead
He stands there and stares and takes in the sound

Of a million legs, amassing like hair
And sees all the baby arachnids there
Crawling towards their father, all unaware
They are the fear of man, his worst nightmare —

The Monstrous Vedette

— To be a film star is my dearest daydream.
Myra Breckinridge, Gore Vidal

I

I'm post-Gutenberg/pre-Apocalypse,
There's nothing — *Cut! Print!* — I won't do for fame!
You'll find me, lips smeared, the blood of the game
Still dripping, my tongue still licking the drips.

I am the black sun. Look up! The eclipse
Radiates decadence — I do the same!
My constellation, my star is aflame
I'm worshiped, or will be, on all the strips!

Retro temples are rising as we speak!
There's blood on the alters and late night screens,
As Art, in all of its artforms, careens

Towards the end of the world — So gross! So chic! —
And I — male, female, pure plural — wink, smile!
Whore of Babylon and the cinephile!

II

When I say, I'd do anything for fame,
I mean, like St. Sebastian, an array
Of trained Roman arrows pointing my way,
I'd cast my gaze upwards, pose for the frame;

And like Joan of Arc, tongues of fire and flame
Teasing up my legs and coarse negligee,
I'd moisten my eyes with tears, and display
My faith in my star and all the acclaim

Destined to come to me, even in death;
For strapped to a tree or tied to a pyre,
My last lines bound up with my final breath,

It's one take and I'm about to expire,
It's my shot at stardom, my lit marquee,
And I know, *all eyes are focused on me…*

Epilogue

A monstrous vedette resides in my mind
Where her voice penetrates me day and night—
Behind my eyes her pinup blocks my sight—
Her songs paralyze me, render me blind —

She's like a siren, not a muse, the wind
Of her tail is hidden beneath the white
Waves of her platinum blond curls and despite
My desperate plea that she be real, I find

The dark fantasy of her bite by far
The most seductive thing since Dante's star—
The most transcendent and the most bizarre—

Are you Myra/Myron? Byron? Beatrice?
What irresistible nightmare is this?
What gross impossibility? What bliss?

What torture this queen's chimerical kiss!

Acknowledgments

Some of the poems in this collection have appeared previously in the following:

Beautiful Tragedies 2: An Anthology of the Darkest Poetry: "The Vampire"

The Horror Zine Magazine, Fall 2021: "Alexandrines in Lafayette Cemetery", "Mankind's Spider"

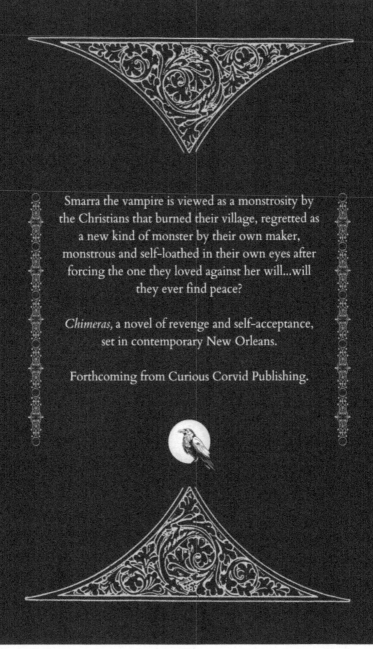

Smarra the vampire is viewed as a monstrosity by the Christians that burned their village, regretted as a new kind of monster by their own maker, monstrous and self-loathed in their own eyes after forcing the one they loved against her will...will they ever find peace?

Chimeras, a novel of revenge and self-acceptance, set in contemporary New Orleans.

Forthcoming from Curious Corvid Publishing.